Fibre Channel
for Mass Storage

ISBN 0-13-010222-9

90000

9 780130 102225

Hewlett-Packard® Professional Books

Atchison	Object-Oriented Test & Management Software Development in C++
Blinn	Portable Shell Programming
Blommers	Architecting Enterprise Solutions with UNIX Networking
Blommers	Practical Planning for Network Growth
Caruso	Power Programming in HP OpenView
Chew	The Java/C++ Cross-Reference Handbook
Cook	Building Enterprise Information Architectures
Costa	Planning and Designing High Speed Networks
Crane	A Simplified Approach to Image Processing
Day	The Color Scanning Handbook
Derickson	Fiber Optic Test and Measurement
Eisenmann and Eisenmann	Machinery Malfunction Diagnosis and Correction
Fernandez	Configuring the Common Desktop Environment
Fristrup	USENET: Netnews for Everyone
Fristrup	The Essential Web Surfer Survival Guide
Gann	Desktop Scanners: Image Quality
Grady	Practical Software Metrics for Project Management and Process Improvement
Greenberg	A Methodology for Developing and Deploying Internet and Intranet Solutions
Grosvenor, Ichiro, O'Brien	Mainframe Downsizing to Upsize Your Business: IT-Preneuring
Gunn	A Guide to NetWare® for UNIX®
Helsel	Graphical Programming: A Tutorial for HP VEE
Helsel	Visual Programming with HP VEE, Third Edition
Holman, Lund	Instant JavaScript
Kane	PA-RISC 2.0 Architecture
Knouse	Practical DCE Programming
Lee	The ISDN Consultant
Lewis	The Art & Science of Smalltalk
Lichtenbelt, Crane, Naqvi	Introduction to Volume Rendering
Loomis	Object Databases in Practice
Lucke	Designing and Implementing Computer Workgroups
Lund	Integrating UNIX® and PC Network Operating Systems
Madell	Disk and File Management Tasks on HP-UX
Mahoney	High-Mix Low-Volume Manufacturing
Malan, Letsinger, Coleman	Object-Oriented Development at Work: Fusion In the Real World
McFarland	X Windows on the World
McMinds/Whitty	Writing Your Own OSF/Motif Widgets
Norton, DiPasquale	Thread Time: The Multithreaded Programming Guide
Orzessek, Sommer	ATM: & MPEG-2: A Practical Guide to Computer Security
Phaal	LAN Traffic Management
Pipkin	Halting the Hacker: A Practical Guide to Computer Security
Poniatowski	HP-UX 11.x System Administration "How To" Book, Second Edition
Poniatowski	HP NetServer Guide for Windows NT®
Poniatowski	HP-UX System Administration Handbook and Toolkit
Poniatowski	HP-UX 10.x System Administration "How To" Book
Poniatowski	Learning the HP-UX Operating System
Poniatowski	Windows NT® and HP-UX System Administrator's "How To" Book
Ryan	Distributed Object Technology: Concepts and Applications
Simmons	Software Measurement: A Visualization Toolkit
Sperley	Enterprise Data Warehouse, Volume 1: Planning, Building, and Implementation
Thomas	Cable Television Proof-of-Performance
Thomas, Edgington	Digital Basics for Cable Television Systems
Thornburgh	Fibre Channel for Mass Storage
Weygant	Clusters for High Availability: A Primer of HP-UX Solutions
Witte	Electronic Test Instruments
Yawn, Stachnick, Sellars	The Legacy Continues: Using the HP 3000 with HP-UX and Windows NT

Fibre Channel
for Mass Storage

Ralph H. Thornburgh

http://www.hp.com/go/retailbooks

Prentice Hall PTR
Upper Saddle River, NJ 07458
www.phptr.com

Library of Congress Cataloging-in-Publication Data

Thornburgh, Ralph H.
    Fibre channel for mass storage / Ralph H. Thornburgh.
        p.   cm. -- (Hewlett-Packard professional books)
    Includes bibliographical references and index.
    ISBN 0-13-010222-9
    1. Fibre Channel (Standard) 2. Computer storage devices.
    I. Title. II. Series.
    TK7895.B87.T48 1999
    004.6'6--dc21
                                   99-24516
                                    CIP

Editorial/production supervision: *Nicholas Radhuber*
Manufacturing manager: *Alexis Heydt*
Acquisitions editor: *Jill Pisoni*
Marketing manager: *Lisa Konzelmann*
Cover design: *Talar Agasyon*
Cover design director: *Jerry Votta*
Manager, Hewlett-Packard Retail Publishing: *Patricia Pekary*
Editor, Hewlett-Packard Retail Publishing: *Susan Wright*

Comments? Write to HP Retail Publishing at bookreview@hp.com.

© 1999 by Hewlett-Packard Company
Published by Prentice Hall PTR
Prentice-Hall, Inc.
Upper Saddle River, New Jersey 07458

Printed in the United States of America
10 9 8 7 6 5 4 3 2

ISBN 0-13-010222-9

Prentice-Hall International (UK) Limited, *London*
Prentice-Hall of Australia Pty. Limited, *Sydney*
Prentice-Hall Canada Inc., *Toronto*
Prentice-Hall Hispanoamericana, S.A., *Mexico*
Prentice-Hall of India Private Limited, *New Delhi*
Prentice-Hall of Japan, Inc., *Tokyo*
Prentice-Hall (Singapore) Pte.Ltd., *Singapore*
Editora Prentice-Hall do Brasil, Ltda., *Rio de Janeiro*

Contents

Chapter 1: Overview of Fibre Channel for Mass Storage 1

Chapter 2: Fibre Channel Functional Levels and Protocols 13

Chapter 3: Fibre Channel Arbitrated Loop (FC-AL) 35

Glossary 119

Bibliography 127

Index 129

List of Figures

Preface

WHAT THIS BOOK IS ABOUT

This book discusses the implementation of Fibre Channel technology for Mass Storage environments. It opens with discussions on storage architectures, their limitations, and how Fibre Channel helps to overcome these limitations.

Next, details of the Fibre Channel technology, focused on the mass storage application, are discussed. Addressing schemes for the Hewlett-Packard implementation are covered in detail as well as Hewlett-Packard products supporting this technology. And finally, future developments and improvements are addressed.

WHO SHOULD READ THIS BOOK?

You should read this book if Fibre Channel is new to you or if you will be working with peripherals that are attached to a Hewlett-Packard system using Fibre Channel technology. This is a brand new technology that is quickly becoming an industry standard. It is already being installed in data centers around the world and may very well be the next communications protocol installed at your location.

If you are a System Administrator and your job is to control configurations and resources of computer systems or do installation of peripherals, this book is a must. If you are a Network Administrator and your job is to configure and support networks, this book is a must. Also read this book if you are a Technical Support Technician and you support or troubleshoot computer systems and their resources.

WHY IS THIS BOOK NEEDED?

Fibre Channel is a new technology and many people are not familiar with its functionality or terminology. Therefore, this book was written to introduce new Fibre Channel users to this important, fast rising technology.

Publications that do exist on Fibre Channel, talk more generically about the technology or focus on the networking aspects. This publication is focused on adding information on Fibre Channel as a technology applied to the mass storage environment and specifically how Hewlett-Packard is implementing Fibre Channel in mass storage environments.

HOW TO USE THIS BOOK

This book can and should be used as a reference book. For example, if you are familiar with Fibre Channel you would want to review the functional levels in Chapter Two and then read on from there. If you are familiar with Fibre Channel and only want to know how HP is implementing addressing, you could read Chapter Four. However, if you are unfamiliar with Fibre Channel you will want to start at the beginning, including this preface, and read through chapter by chapter. It is written in a progressive manner to lead you through learning step-by-step.

AT A GLANCE

Following is a chapter-by-chapter glance at this book:

Chapter 1 — This chapter discusses limitations of current mass storage architectures, explains how Fibre Channel answers these limitations, and defines basic terms and topologies.

Chapter 2 — This chapter details the functional levels of Fibre Channel, emphasizing physical components. There are six levels, three are port levels and three are node levels.

Chapter 3 — This chapter discusses the features and operations of the Fibre Channel Arbitrated Loop (FC-AL), and explains how FC-AL is a very effective topology for mass storage. Hewlett-Packard has a commitment to this topology, as evidenced by its Fibre Channel hub product. This chapter will familiarize the reader with the characteristics, operations, and advantages of FC-AL.

Chapter 4 — This chapter explains why Fibre Channel is a fast, flexible technology that enables a large number of devices to communicate. This chapter describes in detail Peripheral Device, Logical Unit, and Volume Set addressing, which is unique to Hewlett-Packard's HP-UX Operating System environment.

Chapter 5 — This chapter presents an overview of the Hewlett-Packard's Fibre Channel products, describes the systems that support Fibre Channel, and discusses how the products work together.

Chapter 6 — This chapter discusses the future developments and improvements to Fibre Channel and how to get more information. This chapter familiarizes the reader with some of the capabilities that may become available in the near future.

Acknowledgements

I would like to acknowledge the following people for their efforts and work they have accomplished for the Fibre Channel initiative within Hewlett-Packard.

Kyle Black — for his technical reviews of this material during development.

Paul McGowan — for his support while writing this book and for his technical reviews of the material.

Maris Montanet — for her work writing product service manuals and an HP *Journal* article introducing Fibre Channel.

Judy Smith — for her work writing training manuals for the HP Fibre Channel field training and an HP *Journal* article introducing the Hewlett-Packard Fibre Channel chip.

Debbie Clingingsmith — for her work writing and delivering the HP Fibre Channel field training material.

Russ Routh — for his work on the HP Fibre Channel Arbitrated Loop Hub.

Barry Schoenborn — for all his efforts and support during the development of the HP Fibre Channel field training material and this book.

Bobbi Gibson — the Information Engineering department manager for supporting me in my efforts to write this book.

Jade Simonson — the Technical Marketing manager of our division for supporting me in my efforts to write this book.

About the Author

Ralph Thornburgh has worked for Hewlett-Packard Company for 24 years as an IT trainer, IT Data Center Manager, and Learning Products Engineer (technical writer).

During that time he has created twenty-one training classes for Hewlett-Packard data center employees and support personnel worldwide. He has also written fifteen user manuals and numerous technical support manuals.

He lead the team that wrote the multicourse training program for Hewlett-Packard's implementation of Fibre Channel for Mass Storage and two other classes for Hewlett-Packard Fibre Channel peripheral devices.

While at Hewlett-Packard, Ralph held a secondary teaching certificate for three years. He designed and delivered computer class curriculum, to include operating systems and computer operations, for The Computer Learning Center in Santa Clara, California.

Ralph has also designed, developed, and delivered an American Sign Language (ASL) course for middle-school children.

Ralph was also in the U.S. Army for eleven years, part of which was spent in the California Army National Guard. There he was the section training sergeant, training soldiers in technical skills such as Aviation Electrician, as well as in Basic Combat Skills, such as land navigation (map reading) and basic marksmanship.

Overview of Fibre Channel for Mass Storage

This chapter discusses:

- Limitations of current mass storage architectures
- How Fibre Channel answers these limitations
- Basic terms and topologies

1.1 Current Mass Storage Architectures

Current architectures (data transfer protocols) have three major problems:

1. Limited speed
2. Limited distance between devices
3. Limited number of devices supported

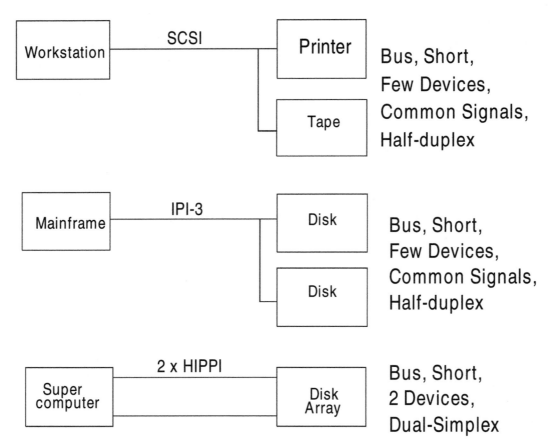

Figure 1-1   Current Limitations

For example, the small Computer System Interface (SCSI) parallel interface is restricted to:

- the bus being no longer than 25 meters
- 32 SCSI devices per bus
- a double cable system

In today's modern computer system environments, these restrictions are very limiting to design and confining in space, and it gets worse. The two-byte wide SCSI P-cable limits configurations to 16 devices.

The single-ended SCSI protocol is limited to eight IDs or addresses per bus (seven devices and one controller), and wide differential SCSI is limited to 16 IDs per bus (15 devices and one controller) to configure a one-terabyte disk storage unit. A fully redundant disk array would require 30 SCSI IDs (two per bus).

These concerns about limited speed, distance, and number of devices caused the industry to start thinking about alternatives. The alternative is Fibre Channel.

1.2 What is Fibre Channel?

Fibre Channel is a new communications protocol designed to overcome the limitations of existing architectures. It is a generic data transport mechanism with the primary task of transporting data at the fastest rate possible using current technology. Fibre Channel is a scalable interface for achieving high-speed data transfer rates among heterogeneous systems and peripherals. System types could include supercomputers, mainframes, workstations, and desktops, (personal computers).

Peripherals could include mass storage devices such as disk arrays and possibly tape libraries. The main purpose of Fibre Channel is to have any number of existing protocols over a variety of physical media and existing cable options. The following table demonstrates the various speeds that can be attained using the different cable types.

Table 1-1

Type/ Speed (Mhz)	Single Mode @9 um	Multi-mode @50 um	Multi-mode @62.5 um	Co-ax	Mini-co-ax	Twinax	STP
133				100 m	42 m	93 m	80 m
266	1300 nm @ 10 km	780 nm @ 2 km	780 nm @ 1 km	100 m	28 m	66 m	57 m
533	1300 nm @ 10 km	780 nm @ 1 km	780 nm @ 1 km	71 m	19 m	46 m	46 m
1063	1300 nm @ 10 km	780 nm @ 500 m	780 nm @ 175 m	50 m	14 m	33 m	28 m
2125	1300 nm @ 2 km	780 nm @ 500 m					
4250	1300 nm @ 2 km	780 nm @ 175 m					

1.2.1 Fibre Channel for Networking

Fibre Channel can be used for networking. The Fibre Channel standard was written to also cover networking protocols (system-to-system communication). Hewlett-Packard's networking implementation uses a speed of 25 Megabytes per second, (M/bytes/s, also known as Mbps) or 266 (265.625) megabaud. This is also known as quarter speed, with full speed being 100 Mbytes/s or 1063 (1062.5) megabaud. Full speed is also known as gigabit speed. Consult the publications listed in Section 6.2 for more information on Fibre Channel as applied to the networking environment.

1.3 Fibre Channel for Mass Storage

Since Fibre Channel is a generic data transport mechanism, Fibre Channel can transmit a number of existing networking and I/O protocols:

I/O protocols:
- SCSI
- HIPPI
- IPI

Network protocols:
- IP
- IEEE 802.2

Hewlett-Packard has chosen to support the SCSI-3 protocol over Fibre Channel for its mass storage environment. Mass storage consists of several device classes:

- tapes
- disks
- disk arrays

1.4 Advantages of Fibre Channel for Mass Storage

There are some definite advantages to using Fibre Channel over other architectures. Although this is not an all-inclusive list, these are the major advantages:

1.4.1 Distance

Hewlett-Packard supports up to 10,000 meters (10km) between the computer (or system) and the peripheral. What this means is that between the computer and the peripheral there can be a distance of 10 kilometers. The next section, "Topologies," will describe this in more detail, however, the distance advantage is an excellent solution for the campus-type environment.

1.4.2 Speed

Fibre Channel permits a theoretical speed of up to 4000 Mbps. (As mentioned previously Hewlett Packard supports 1063 Mbps.) Speeds depend greatly on the design of the pieces and parts that are connected within the topology between the computer and the peripheral. Our challenge within the industry now is to determine how to achieve these higher speeds allowed by the Fibre Channel standard. This speaks directly to performance because with the speeds capable with Fibre Channel throughput increases by four or five times over current channels.

1.4.3 Connectivity or Scalability

Computer system environments today are very limited in the number of devices that can be connected together. They are also limited in that today's configurations do not easily allow the introduction of new technologies, protocols, or even different protocols simultaneously.

Fibre Channel addresses these issues by allowing:

- from two to over 16 million ports that can be concurrently logged in to a Fabric with the 24-bit address identifier
- for the introduction of new technologies like laser light
- for the transportation of different protocols simultaneously

1.5 Basic Terms

A set of new terms having no previous association with other protocols has been defined for Fibre Channel. For example, SCSI has Initiators and Targets, and Fibre Channel has Originators and Responders. In Fibre Channel, the Originators are devices that originate (initiate) a transaction or operation. The Responders then, answer the operation of the Originators. Also refer to the glossary in the back of this book for complete definitions of all terms.

The following pages will describe more words, as well as the names of some of the pieces and parts of Fibre Channel technology/topologies. A node is a device. A device is any processor or mass storage subsystem with Fibre Channel functionality. A node has at least one port (N_Port, the 'N' stands for node) and can have multiple ports. A port is the connecting interface between the cable and the device, located on the device. The cable is referred to as the link. Fibre Channel is based on full duplex operation, therefore two fibers, (TX and RX) one to transmit and one to receive, are required to operate a port. The term fiber in this case can be a copper cable or an optical strand cable.

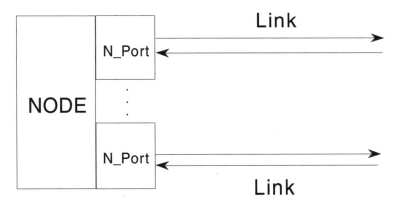

Figure 1-2   Basic Terms

1.6 Topologies

1.6.1 Point-to-Point

The first topology to discuss is the simplest, it is called a point-to-point topology. It is two nodes (devices) connected together. One node could be a computer system and the other node could be a disk array.

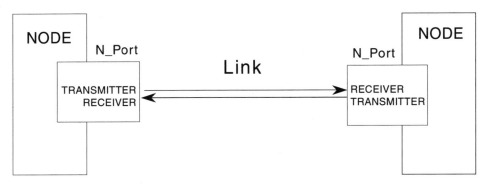

Figure 1-3   Point-to-Point Topology

This particular topology uses two nodes (each node must have at least one port), and the nodes are connected using one link or cable. The point-to-point connection guarantees instant access with no interference from any other node or application.

If a peripheral node, such as a disk array, has two N_Ports, access to the disk array could be shared between two computer systems. For example, the disk array could act as a repository of common software for two computer systems. This would be considered two point-to-point connections. See Figure 1-4.

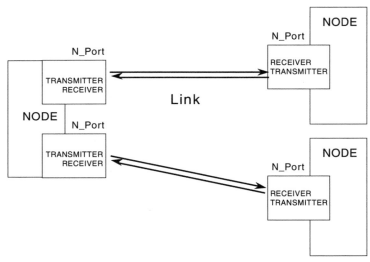

Figure 1-4   Two Point-to-Point Connections

A point-to-point connection may also be considered a two-node loop. Hewlett-Packard's implementation of point-to-point is a two-node loop. This brings us to our next topology to be discussed.

1.6.2 Arbitrated Loop

A loop, called Fibre Channel Arbitrated Loop (FC-AL) can have up to 127 ports connected in series (one right after the other) continuing around and back to the originator. For example, the node 1 transmitter is connected to the node 2 receiver, the node 2 transmitter is connected to the node 3 receiver and so on until the final node transmitter is connected to the node 1 receiver, thus completing the loop. Figure 1-5 illustrates this example.

A node loop port (NL_Port) wins arbitration on the loop and establishes a connection with another NL_Port on the loop. At the time the connection is established it is considered to be a point-to-point connection or two-node loop.

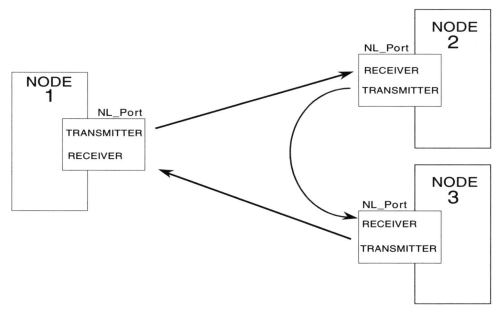

Figure 1-5   Arbitrated Loop Topology

In an arbitrated loop only the two connected ports can communicate at any given time. All the other ports act as repeaters. When the communication comes to an end between the two connected ports, the loop becomes available for arbitration and a new connection may be established. Fairness is provided for during arbitration to provide equal access to all ports. The FC-AL features, operations, and Hewlett-Packard's implementation will be discussed in further detail in Chapter 3.

1.6.3 Switch Topology or Fabric

The switch topology uses the concept of fabric. The fabric is a mesh of connections. When attached to a fabric, a single N_Port can access all the rest, including members of loops.

Unlike the FC-AL topology, many connections may be established within the fabric. It can be compared to a telephone system where many phone calls may be occurring all at the same time.

Any node can be attached to a fabric through the N or NL_ports by way of a link. The port in the fabric is called an F_Port. An N_Port attaches to an F_Port. If an NL_Port is attached to a fabric, then the fabric port is an FL_Port.

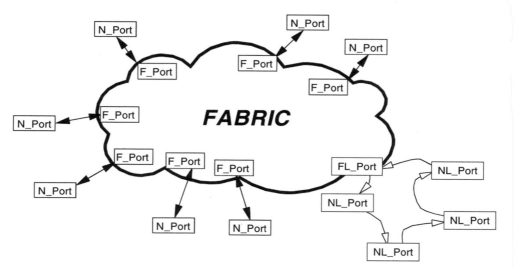

Figure 1-6   Fabric Topology

1.6.4 A Typical Campus Topology

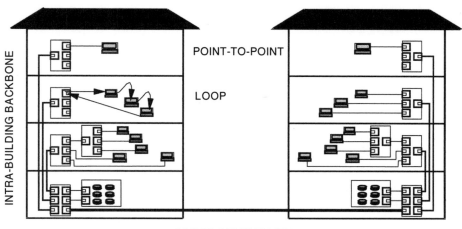

Figure 1-7   Typical Fibre Channel Campus Topology

A campus topology is nothing more than cabling buildings together so data can be transferred from a computer system in one building to storage devices, whether they be disk storage or tape storage for backup or some other devices, in another building.

Using current technology these buildings could be up to 10,000 meters from each other. This type of topology would incorporate the use of two long-wave hubs attached by way of a 9 micron (um) cable. Providing the cable has a measured signal strength loss of less than 9 db.

CHAPTER . 2

Fibre Channel Functional Levels and Protocols

This chapter discusses:

- **Functional levels of Fibre Channel**
    - **FC-0 Level — Physical**
    - **FC-1 Level — Encode/Decode**
    - **FC-2 Level — Framing protocol/Flow control**
    - **FC-3 Level — Common services**
    - **FC-4 Level — Protocol mapping**

- **Upper Level Protocols**
- **Physical components**
- **Classes of service**

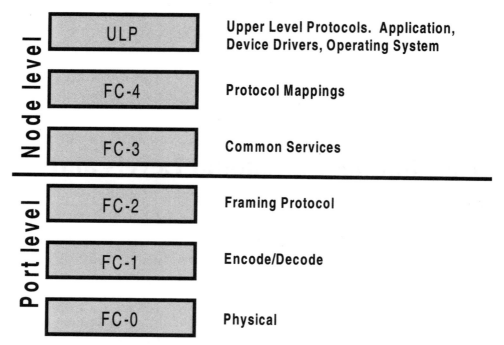

Figure 2-1   Fibre Channel Protocol Functional Levels

2.1 Functional Levels

Fibre Channel Protocol (FCP) functional levels are FC-0 through FC-4. The FC-3 and FC-4 levels are outside the port level, permitting the sharing of resources of several ports in the event of future extensions. Applications lie above the FC-4 level. For example, the peripheral drivers for a SCSI application that typically communicates with Host Bus Adapters (HBAs) will communicate with the FC-4 level.

2.1.1 Placement in a Topology

As shown in Figure 2-1, FC-0, FC- , and FC-2 are implemented at the port level. FC-3, FC-4, and the Upper Level Protocols (ULPs) are implemented at the node level. Fibre Channel considers that which is not visible on the link (above the FC-0 physical level) to be system dependent, and simply identifies the functions to be performed. It does not require allocation or placement.

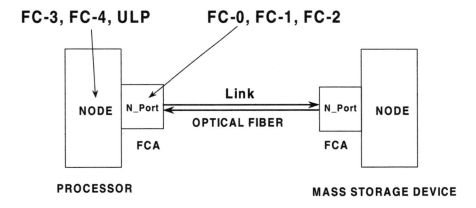

Figure 2-2   Placement in a Topology

Figure 2-2 shows an example of a simple point-to-point (two-node loop) topology to identify where the functionality of each level resides. FC-0, FC-1, and FC-2 are all implemented at the Port level. This means that each Port has the functionality of these levels. FC-3, FC-4, and ULPs are all implemented at the Node level.

Figure 2-3 shows another way to demonstrate this. The horizontal line in the middle divides the Node from the Port. You will see something new in this Figure. Where there are multiples of FC-0, FC-1, and FC-2, there is only one FC-3, the common services level. That is because the FC-3 functionality may interact with multiple ports on a node. And then again above the FC-3 level, there are multiple FC-4s and ULPs. That is because there may be multiple ULPs within a node which map through multiple FC-4s.

Figure 2-4 shows yet another example. This Figure clearly shows that there are five levels used by Fibre Channel, (FC-0 through FC-4) separating the Upper Level Protocols into the system interface. Also, you can see that FC-4 can accommodate not only the channel protocols of SCSI, IPI and others, but can also accommodate network protocols like IEEE 802.2.

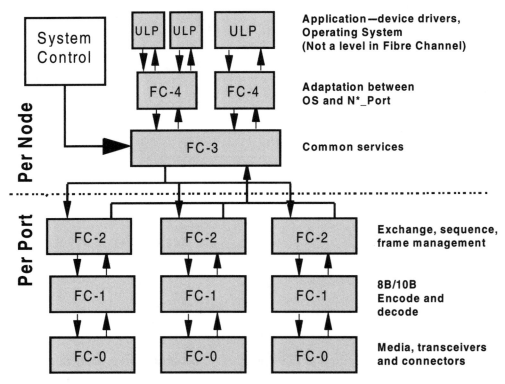

Figure 2-3   Functional Levels

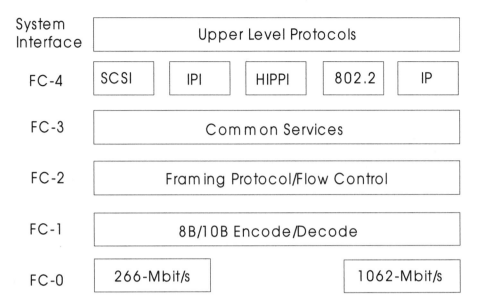

Figure 2-4   Fibre Channel Framing levels

Now you have a good overview of the different functional levels within Fibre Channel. Continue on to the next section to read about the detailed characteristics of each level.

2.2 FC-0: The Physical Layer

Level FC-0 deals with the physical variants:
- fiber
- connectors
- receivers
- data encoders/decoders
- serializers/deserializers
- transmitters

FC-0 deals strictly with the serial bit stream to be sent and received, and the conductors used to transmit that stream. This layer is called the physical layer. The Fibre Channel standard calls this function the Link Control Facility (LCF). The requirements are different for different types of media and different data rates.

2.2.1 Connectors

Remember, Chapter 1 stated that the main purpose of Fibre Channel is to have any number of existing protocols over a variety of physical media and existing cable options. Therefore, FC-0 provides for four types of connectors to accommodate for the variety of physical media and for possible existing cable.

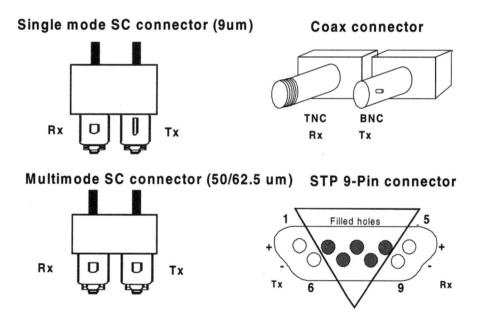

Figure 2-5 FC-0 Connectors

The single mode and multimode connectors connect to fiber optic cable. Single mode fiber optic cable is thinner and has less bandwidth than multimode cable. Therefore, single mode cable is used for long distance transmissions, 10,000 meters (10km), where as multimode cable is used for shorter distances, 500 meters.

In that case then, an example for use might be to connect two buildings some distance away from each other with single mode fiber optic cable. Then, within each building, connect each floor using multimode cable.

A word of caution, when working in a mixed environment of single and multimode cabling, be aware that the connectors have been keyed to prevent accidental connection of single mode to multimode or the reverse. However, the keying of the connectors is not perfect nor completely standardized. Also, multimode fiber cable does not work with single mode transmitters and receivers. The single mode light "rattles around" in the big 50 or 62.5 um fibers and dissipates quickly, causing data loss.

Currently, Hewlett-Packard only supports fiber optic cable with its use of Fibre Channel and therefore only uses the SC connectors shown in Figure 2-5.

The Fibre Channel standard does provide for connections to co-ax and copper cabling.

For co-ax cable:

• the TNC for receive
• the BNC for transmit

For copper cable the shielded twisted-pair (STP), 9-pin D-type connector (DB9), is used. To prevent accidental attachments, the middle five holes in the Fibre Channel DB9 female connector are filled.

2.2.2 Fiber Optic Cables

Figure 2-6 shows a typical fiber cable and its major components. The light travels through the core, the smallest component. The core is covered, or surrounded, by a material called cladding. Its purpose is to keep the light in the core, not let it escape.

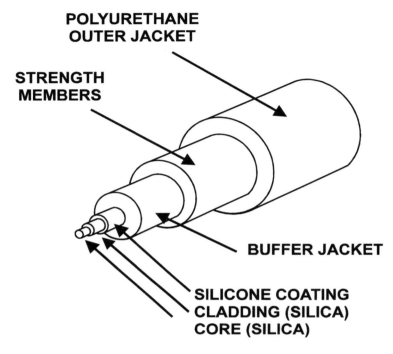

Figure 2-6   Fiber Cable Components

Then the cladding is wrapped by a coating which is in turn wrapped by the buffer jacket. This is all done so the light stays within the core. However, the core fiber itself is very thin and fragile. Therefore to give strength to the cable and more protection to the core fiber, the buffer jacket is wrapped with a strengthening material. Finally, all of these layers of fiber and material are wrapped with the polyurethane outer jacket. Fiber cable is not subject to electromagnetic interference, and since the data is transmitted by light it is secure from eavesdropping.

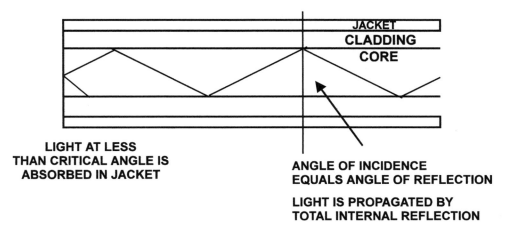

Figure 2-7   Light Transmission

Figure 2-7 demonstrates how light travels through the core. It is reflected from side to side. This also shows the cladding keeping the light in the core.

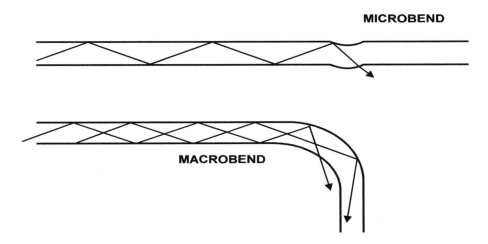

Figure 2-8   Bend Radius

Figure 2-8 shows what happens when the bend radius of fiber cable is exceeded. The maximum bend radius is 3 cm. If the cabling is bent beyond 3 cm, data loss or data corruption is likely to occur. The core fiber may also crack or break.

2.2.2.1 OFC and non-OFC

Open Fibre Control (OFC) is a safety feature used to prohibit the laser light from functioning when there is a break or disconnect in the fiber cable. This is used specifically with high intensity laser lights. Hewlett-Packard uses non-OFC because the lasers are of low intensity. Therefore, the laser light is not turned off when there is a disconnect. However, this does not mean you should look at or point the fiber cable directly at your eye, since there still could be some damage. When checking a fiber cable to see if a laser light exists, point the cable end at a white piece of paper. If a red dot appears on the paper, then the transmitting laser is functioning.

2.2.2.2 Wavelength

Wavelength is a topic related to single and multimode connectors. Long wave lasers are used for long Fibre Channel links, from approximately 500 to 10,000 meters. They are typically used with single mode fiber of a 9-micron core size.

Short wave lasers are used for FC-AL links up to approximately 500 meters. They are typically used with multimode fiber. The preferred fiber core size is 50-micron. 62.5-micron core size is also supported for compatibility with existing FDDI installations. However, fiber of this type has smaller bandwidth and, in this case, the distance is limited by the fiber bandwidth. The length recommendation for the 62.5-micron fiber cable is 175 meters.

When pulling new cable, it is recommended that the customer pull both 9- and 50-micron cable to accommodate future expansion.

2.3 FC-1: The Transmission Protocol Level

The FC-1 level defines the transmission protocol including the 8B/10B encode/decode scheme, byte synchronization, and character-level error control. This protocol uses the 8B/10B encoding scheme that encodes 8-bit bytes into 10-bit transmission characters. The 8B/10B encoding was developed by IBM and was determined to be the best for the expected error rate of the system.

The 8B/10B code has outstanding line characteristics including long transmission distances and very good error-detection capability. The 8B/10B code finds errors that a parity check cannot detect. Parity does not find even numbers of bit errors, only odd numbers. But 8B/10B finds almost all errors. Fibre Channel also employs a Cyclic Redundancy Check (CRC) on transmitted data. This also assists with error detection.

To assist with transmission the 8B/10B code uses 12 special characters. However, we are only concerned with one, the 28.5 special character. At present, it is the only special character used by Fibre Channel in the 8B/10B code.

2.3.1 8B/10B Encoding

The format of the 8B/10B character is *Ann.m*, where:
- *A* is equal to "D" for data or "K" for a special character
- *nn* is the decimal value of the lower five bits of a byte (bits EDCBA)
- "." is a period
- *m* is the decimal value of the upper three bits of a byte (bits HGF)

Figure 2-9 shows the translation of the HEX number 45.

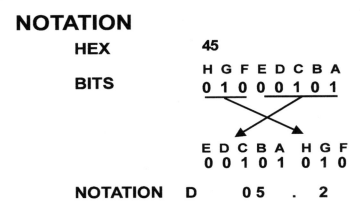

Figure 2-9 8B/10B Encoding

The 8B/10B encoded bytes have a property know as "disparity," which can be positive, negative, or neutral. An 8B/10B byte has negative disparity if there are more binary ones in the byte than binary zeroes. Conversely, the byte has positive disparity if there are more binary zeroes than ones. Neutral disparity is when the number of binary ones equals the number of binary zeroes.

2.3.2 K28.5 Special Character Encoding

The *K28.5* special character has the following components:

• K stands for special character
• 28 is the decimal value of bits EDCBA -- 11100
• "." is a period
• 5 is the decimal value of bits HGF -- 101

Figure 2-10 shows the translation of the HEX number BC.

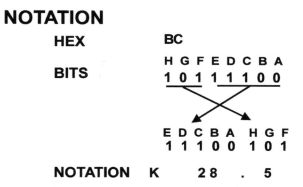

NOTATION

HEX	BC

BITS	H G F E D C B A 1 0 1 1 1 1 0 0

EDCBA HGF
1 1 1 0 0 1 0 1

NOTATION   K   2 8   .   5

TRANSMISSION ORDER

8B/10B	A B C D E F G H
	a b c d e i f g h j
	0 0 1 1 1 1 0 1 0 **(RD-)**
OR	1 1 0 0 0 0 0 1 0 1 **(RD+)**

Figure 2-10   8B/10B Translation

2.3.3 FC-1 Transmission Word

A transmission word is composed of four transmission characters. Remember, the 8B/10B code encoded an 8-bit byte into a 10-bit character. Therefore, a transmission word is a 40-bit group of four 10B transmission characters. A transmission word can be one of two kinds:

- data—the first transmission character is an encoded data byte
- ordered set—the forth transmission character is the K28.5 special character

If the transmission word is data, each of the four transmission characters is an encoded data byte.

If the transmission word is an ordered set, the first byte is a K28.5 transmission character. The other three transmission characters are normal encoded data bytes. Ordered sets permit control functions to be imbedded in the bit stream. One simple use of ordered sets is to determine at a receiver where word boundaries are. If all transmission words are data transmission words, the receiver has only a 2.5% chance of getting it right (that is, one in 40 bits).

2.3.4 FC-1: Ordered Set

An ordered set is a transmission word beginning with a special character, as previously discussed, the K28.5 character. Because this special character is present, this transmission word has a special control function meaning. There are three possible meanings:

- Frame delimiter—This defines what class of service is required. (Classes of service will be explained later in this chapter.) The frame contains a start of frame (SOF) and an end of frame (EOF) delimiter.
- Primitive signals—There are two kinds of primitive signals:
  - The ordered set may be a primitive signal used for buffer-to-buffer flow control.
  - There is an ordered set for idle primitives. Idles are words that fill the space between frames. In Fibre Channel, the transmitter must continuously send something over the media. This helps preserve bit, byte, and word synchronization, and permits faster communication.
- Primitive sequences—A set of three identical ordered sets for link control. These are used for notification of link failures and loss of synchronization.

2.4 FC-2: Framing Protocol

The FC-2 framing protocol manages flow control so data will be delivered with no collisions or loss. This level defines the signaling protocol, including the frame and byte structure, which is the data transport mechanism used by Fibre Channel. The framing protocol is used to break sequences into individual frames for transmission, flow control, 32-bit CRC generation, and various classes of service.

To aid in data transfer, FC-2 provides for the following elements:

- Frames—basic units of information transfer. The maximum payload of a frame is 2112 bytes.

- Sequences—are made up of one or more frames. FC-2 names each sequence and tracks it to completion.

- Exchanges—are the largest construct understood by FC-2. An exchange is a unidirectional or bidirectional set of nonconcurrent sequences. SCSI-3 FCP uses bidirectional exchanges, with information passing in one direction at a time. To send data in the opposite direction, sequence initiative is passed from one port to another and back again. Each port generates one or more sequences within the exchange.

- Packets—are made up of one or more exchanges.

2.4.1 Frame Structure

The following figure demonstrates frame structure.

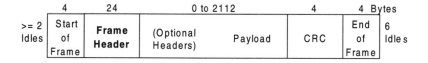

Figure 2-11 FC-2 Frame Structure

The total length of the frame is 2148 transmission characters or 537 transmission words. The SOF, CRC, and EOF are all one transmission word in length with the frame header being six transmission words in length. The frame is followed by a minimum of 6 idles (or 24 transmission characters).

2.4.2 Frame Header Structure

The frame header is divided into fields to carry control information. The following figure shows these fields.

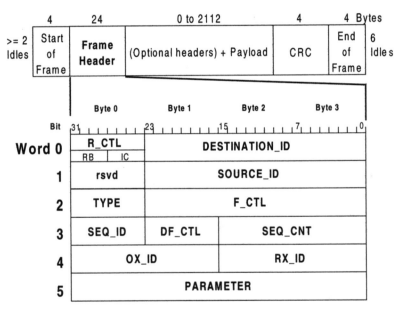

Figure 2-12   Frame Header Structure

Table 2-1   Frame Header Structure Explanations

Routing Control (R_CTL)	Contains IC (Information Category) and RB (Routing Bits) subfields. Routing Bits indicate the frame type. The IC field indicates payload content (for example, SCSI status).
Destination ID (D_ID)	The native address of the destination N_Port, a well-known address, or an alias address.
Source ID (S_ID)	The address identifier of the source N_Port.
Type	The protocol associated with the payload (for example, SCSI-3)
Frame Control (F_CTL)	Bits that identify the transfer of sequence; beginning, middle, or end of sequence; and end of connection.
Data Field Control (DF_CTL)	Indicates the presence of optional headers.
Sequence ID (SEQ_ID)	A unique numeric sequence identifier between two ports.
Sequence Count (SEQ_CNT)	A 16-bit rollover frame counter or frame identifier.
Originator Exchange ID (OX_ID)	A number an exchange originator uses to uniquely identify an exchange.
Responder Exchange ID (RX_ID)	A number like OX_ID, but for the exchange responder.
Parameter	Contents may vary with frame type. Often used as a relative offset of payload contents.

2.5 FC-3: Common Services

The FC-3 level, located at the center of the functional levels, concerns itself with functions spanning multiple N_Ports. The FC-3 level is the single point in the architecture through which all traffic must flow in both directions. The FC-3 level will contain services that are common (available) to all ports on a node.

A node may have several ports. A node may also have several ULPs and FC-4 level mappings. However, there is only one FC-3 Common Services level per node. The FC-3 level can manage a set of tables holding the login information for other active ports. Each port on the FC-3 level knows which ports are busy and which exchanges they are busy with.

Figure 2-12 shows where the FC-3 level fits into the overall scheme of all the Fibre Channel levels.

Currently there are three functions defined within the FC-3 level standard:

- Striping—Used to achieve higher bandwidth. Striping allows multiple links simultaneously and transmits a single information unit across multiple links employing multiple N_Ports in parallel.

- Hunt Groups—Are a group of N_Ports associated with a single node. they permit any N_Port on the node to receive information containing the correct alias identifier.

- Multicast—This can be compared to a broadcast message. It allows a single information unit to be transmitted to multiple N_Ports on a node.

The FC-3 level knows nothing about the topology of Fibre Channel or the physical signaling at the lower levels. This is handled by FC-1 and FC-2 levels. FC-3 understands if there are multiple ports attached to a node and if they may participate in multiport operations like multicasting. Knowing which ports are busy allows the FC-3 level to route exchanges between two N*_Ports and FC-4s.

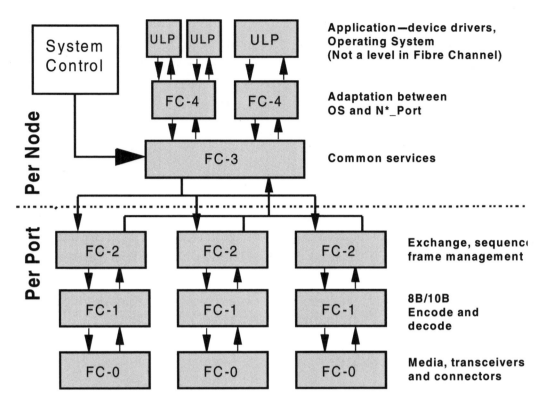

Figure 2-13 FC-3 Common Services Level

2.6 FC-4: Mapping

Mapping is a set of rules that is defined to move information from the Upper Level Protocol interfaces to the lower Fibre Channel levels. the ANSI SCSI committee and the Fibre Channel committees are currently defining these rules.

Currently the rules provide for transforming information units into Fibre Channel sequences and exchanges and back again. When fully developed, these mapping rules are intended to provide clear mapping instructions between the Upper Level Protocol (ULP) and the FC-3 and FC-2 levels to enhance interoperability between applications.

To send data, the FC-4 level takes a unit of information (this is the payload in a frame and is the actual data that is being transmitted, it is referred to as an Information Unit (IU)) from a ULP and transforms it into sequences for the FC-3 and FC-2 levels. To receive data, the FC-4 level takes a sequence from the FC-3 and FC-2 levels and transforms it into an IU for the ULP.

2.7 Upper Level Protocols

The ULPs allow two devices to communicate. For example, a computer sends data to a disk to be stored for later use, or the communication that takes place in a client/server relationship.

There are many standards currently defined that have been in use for years that enable interoperation, such as SCSI or IPI. A goal of Fibre Channel is to provide a structure where legacy ULPs would continue to operate, preserving the software developed in the past. In this regard then, a map will exist in the FC-4 level for every ULP that is transportable over Fibre Channel.

2.8 Classes of Service

Fibre Channel classes of service are managed by the FC-2 level. Currently there are three classes of service defined by the standard:

- Class 1— Dedicated connection service.
    - Connection-oriented
    - Acknowledged delivery
- Class 2— Multiplexed service.
    - Connectionless
    - Acknowledged delivery

• Class 3— Datagram service. This is the current class of service provided for by Hewlett-Packard. The device drivers determine if data is not received and needs to be retransmitted.
- Connectionless
- Unacknowledged delivery

Other classes of service may follow. However, they are currently not defined.

CHAPTER 3

Fibre Channel Arbitrated Loop (FC-AL)

This chapter discusses:

- **FC-AL Characteristics**
    - Types of Loops
- **Operations of the FC-AL**
    - Primitive Signals and Sequences
    - Arbitrated Loop Physical Address
    - Loop States and Operation
- **Hubs**
- **Topologies**

3.1 FC-AL Characteristics

There are three topologies supported by Fibre Channel: loop, point-to-point, and switched. FC-AL is the loop topology that will be discussed here. The FC-AL is a means by which to connect two or more (up to 126) devices in a serial loop configuration. This solution is considered low cost because it does not use hubs and switches in small to medium configurations. It also provides capability to connect to larger loops and fabrics where hubs and switches are used.

In the FC-AL each port discovers when it has been attached to a loop. Addresses are assigned automatically on initialization. Access to the loop is arbitrated, there are no collisions and there is no single permanent loop master.

FC-AL permits fair access on a single arbitrated loop. Access fairness means every port wanting to initiate traffic will have the opportunity to own the loop and initiate traffic before any other port has the opportunity to own the loop for the second time.

3.1.1 Types of Loops

3.1.1.1   FC-AL Private Loop

A private loop is enclosed and known only to itself. Figure 3-1 demonstrates a common configuration used with FC-AL for Fibre Channel Mass Storage. In this example, the processor node only has one Fibre Channel host bus adapter (HBA).

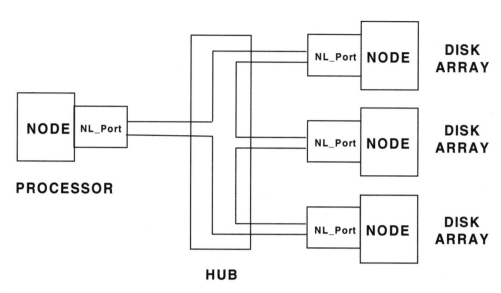

Figure 3-1   FC-AL Private Loop

The processor node is connected to the hub. Then the three devices, in this case disk arrays, are connected to the hub and the loop is formed. If the hub is not used then the connection with all three disk arrays cannot be made. A connection to only one, in point-to-point fashion, could be accomplished. Another option would be to install three HBAs into the processor node and connect each to a disk array separately.

The hub then, provides an advantage in saving HBA slots in the processor node and allows multiple storage devices to be added to the loop. Currently, this is the type of loop configuration Hewlett-Packard supports.

3.1.1.2   FC-AL Public Loop

A Public Loop, shown in Figure 3-2, requires a fabric and has at least one FL_Port connecting to a fabric. A public loop extends the reach of the loop topology by attaching the loop to a fabric. Public loops are a way to leverage the cost of one switched connection over many devices in a loop. Connecting a loop to a fabric is similar to connecting a local area network (LAN) to a wide area network (WAN). The fabric is usually represented by a cloud, as shown in Figure 3-3.

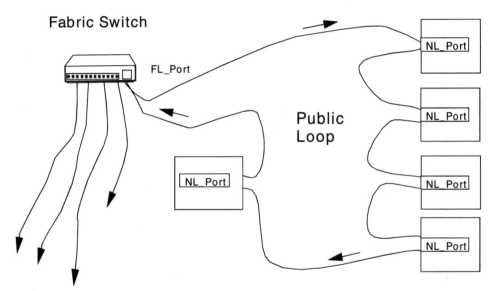

Figure 3-2   FC-AL Public Loop

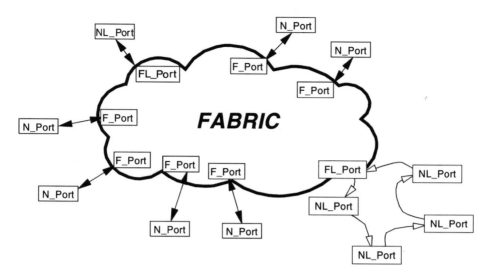

Figure 3-3 FC-AL Fabric

Hewlett-Packard does not currently support public loops or fabrics.

3.2 Operations of the FC-AL

3.2.1 Primitive Signals

Table 3-1   Primitive Signals

Signal	Description
ARB(x)	Arbitrate address x for loop control
OPN(y)	Open one other NL_Port - Full duplex - Half duplex
OPN(r)	Replicate - Broadcast - Selective replicate or multicast
CLS	Close the circuit at the NL_Port
MRK(tx)	Synchronization signal 't' from 'x'

Note:
The 'x' is the address of the port wanting to own the loop and the 'y' is the address of the port to be opened.

Primitive signals are sent by a transmitting port and recognized and acted upon by a receiving port. Currently, the MRK signal is not supported by Hewlett-Packard.

3.2.2 Primitive Sequences

Primitive sequences are not recognized or acted upon until the third consecutive occurrence of the ordered set. Currently, there are only three primitive sequences used:

- LIP Loop Initialization
- LPB Loop Port Bypass
- LPE Loop Port Enable

The LIP sequence allows for discovery of ports on the loop. This means that when a new node is connected to a loop, the LIP sequence discovers it and allows for the new node to be initialized on the loop.

3.2.3 Arbitrated Loop Physical Address (AL-PA)

All ports have a 24-bit native address identifier, called the N_Port ID. The AL-PA is in the lower eight (8) bits of this identifier. The lower the 8-bit address, the higher the priority is for arbitrating. An 8-bit field can have values from 0–255, or 256 values. However, not all of these are used for physical addresses.

AL-PA values must have neutral disparity. (Remember that 8B/10B encoding has positive, negative, or neutral disparity.) There are only 134 neutral disparity values out of the set of 256 8-bit addresses. 126 values, of the 134, are used for port addresses and 8 are used for control functions. Hewlett-Packard uses addresses 00-EF. See Table 3-2 for further reference.

The upper 16 bits are non-zero for public ports on a public loop but are zero for ports on a private loop. This is how the loop determines whether it is talking publicly or privately.

Table 3-2   AL-PA Values

Value	Description
00	Reserved for FL_Port (high priority)
01-EF	Available for active NL_Ports (126 valid neutral disparity values)
F0	Reserved for access fairness algorithm (lowest priority)
F1-F6	Invalid
F7	Used with initialization primitive sequences
F8	Used with initialization primitive sequences
F9-FE	Reserved (3 valid)
FF	Replicate request (low priority) or to address "ALL"

3.2.4 Loop States and Operation

3.2.4.1 Operation Overview

There is a controlled arbitration process for a port to gain control of an arbitrated loop. The Open NL_Port selects a destination NL_Port on the loop before a frame is transmitted. The arbitrating port releases control of the loop when frame transmission is complete.

A port gains ownership of the loop by an arbitration process. The port winning arbitration sends an OPN primitive to the destination node, and enters the Opened state. Upon receiving the OPN primitive, the destination node also enters the Opened state. The loop is now in a point-to-point configuration. Either of the open ports can now send command or data frames.

After completing the information exchange, the port that won arbitration sends a CLS primitive to the destination port. Both ports now return to the monitoring state.

3.2.4.2 The Monitoring State

After port initialization, all ports start in the monitoring state, the loop is idle, no data is being transmitted, and there is no activity. The loop at this time is considered to be closed. While in the monitoring state, ports act as repeaters and are looking for primitive signals and sequences to act upon. Before any port arbitrates for the loop, the loop is filled with Idles.

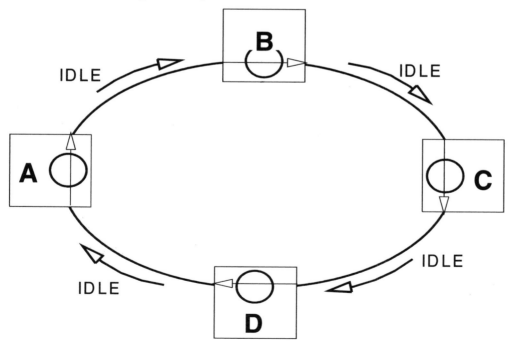

Figure 3-4 Monitoring or Idle State

3.2.4.3 The Arbitration Process

To begin the arbitration process, a port, in this example Port A, sends the primitive signal ARB(a) to notify the loop of its intention to own the loop. Port A wins arbitration when the ARB(a) is returned to it. Receiving its ARB(a) means no higher priority NL_Port needs the loop at this time.

When Port A wants to acquire the loop, there can be different conditions on the loop. For example:

- Some other port may already have control of the loop.
- Several ports may be trying to acquire the loop at the same time.

Port A will win when:

- No other port controls the loop, and
- No port with a lower AL-PA address (higher priority) is arbitrating.

Once a port has acquired the loop, it opens the loop, preventing all other ports from acquiring the loop. It receives and discards all ARB(x) primitive signals.

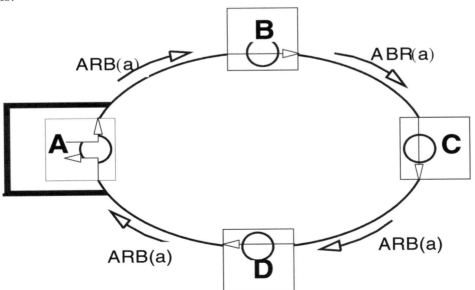

Figure 3-5 Arbitration Process

3.2.4.4   The Open State

In this example, Port A has acquired the loop. It is now in the Open state with the loop physically open at Port A. Nothing may be done until Port A has completed a circuit with its intended destination, in this example, Port C.

Port A sends the OPN primitive signal naming C with an OPN(c,a) for full duplex or an OPN(c,c) for half duplex. Port C is monitoring the loop, acting as a repeater, and listening for any ordered set pertaining to it. Once it receives the OPN primitive signal from Port A, it enters the Open state and physically opens the loop at its port.

The loop is now open between Port A and C and is considered to be a point-to-point connection.

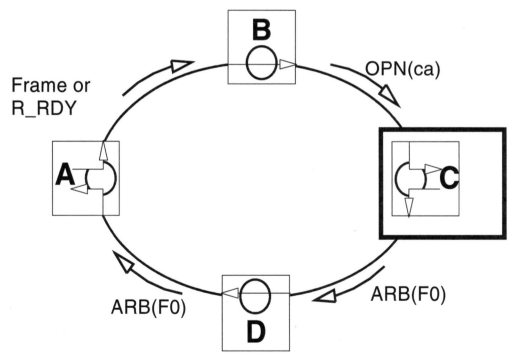

Figure 3-6   The Opened State

3.2.4.5 Open Loop

Both Port A and Port C have opened the loop. Upper level protocol frames and link control frames may now be sent back and forth.

The circuit formed is essentially a point-to-point link between A and C. This is a dedicated path for the duration of the transaction.

Ports B and D are acting as repeaters but are listening for specific ordered sets as before.

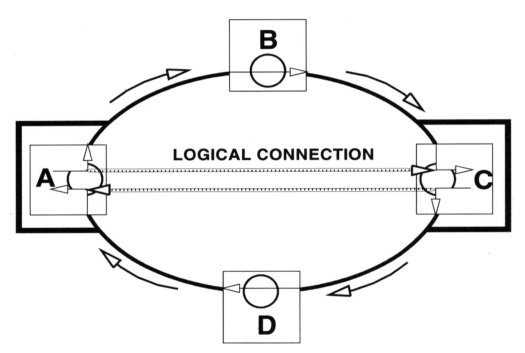

Figure 3-7   Open Loop

3.2.4.6 Closing the Loop

Either one of the Open ports may initiate the closing procedure by sending a CLS primitive signal to the other. In this example, Port A initiates the closing by sending the CLS signal.

Once a port has sent a CLS primitive signal, it may not send frames or R_RDYs. However, it may still receive frames and R_RDYs.

The port receiving the first CLS primitive signal, here, Port C, does not have to close its circuit right away. It may continue to send frames. Once its operation is complete, it sends a CLS primitive signal back to the other port, Port A.

Port C closes when it sends the CLS to Port A and Port A closes when it receives the CLS from Port C. The loop is now closed, with both ports returning to the monitoring state.

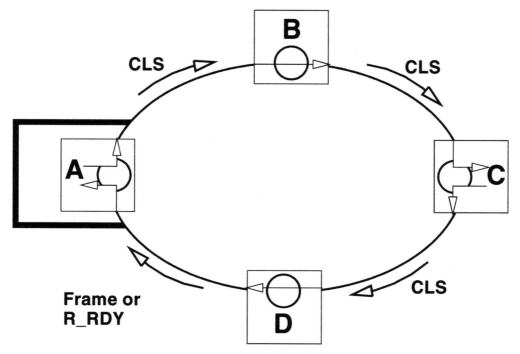

Figure 3-8   Closing the Loop

Once the loop is closed it returns to the state or condition shown in Figure 3-4. There is no activity and all nodes are retransmitting idle signals. When the loop is closed, other ports may acquire the loop.

Access fairness provides other ports on the loop have one chance to acquire the loop before the port that just owned the loop can acquire the loop again. Access fairness does not imply time fairness. In other words, a port may hold on to the loop as long as it is transmitting frames.

3.3 Hubs

Hewlett-Packard's implementation of FC-AL for a private loop includes a hub. FC-AL hubs connect devices to the loop. It is a simple way to connect participants in a private loop. There are two types of hubs:

- Passive, which only reacts to ports being inserted into or removed from a loop
- Active, which are able to do configuration changes dynamically, based on some controlling protocol.

Some hubs can sense or manage configuration changes in the loop, including:

- knowing when NL_Ports are added

- knowing when NL_Ports are removed

- knowing when address changes occur for an entire set of NL_Ports

- switching NL_Ports into or our of a loop

Hubs also provide port bypass circuits to "heal" a loop when a device is removed or fails This allows for less disruption in operations. Hubs help solve the problems of cabling devices and keeping track of which loop a device is on. With central cabling by way of the FC-AL hub, it is easy to add and remove devices from arbitrated loops.

There are some definite advantages to using Fibre Channel hub:

- Extremely fast solution for connecting peripherals and hosts (nodes)
- Up to 124 NL_Ports per loop
- Loop topology eliminates wiring clutter
- FC-AL hubs enhance subsystem availability
- FC-AL hubs provide port bypass circuits to permit "hot" repair

3.4 Topologies

There will be more information about hubs and specifically Hewlett-Packard hubs in Chapter Five. However, for now, to demonstrate a couple of topologies using hubs see Figures 3-9 and 3-10.

3.4.1 Cascading Shortwave Hubs

A server with an FC-AL, short-wave host bus adapter (HBA) can connect to an FC-AL hub 500 meters away. Each of the 10 ports on the hub can connect to an FC-AL device up to 500 meters away.

Cascaded hubs use one port on each hub for the hub-to-hub connection and this increases the potential distance between nodes in the loop an additional 500 meters. In this topology the overall distance is 1500m. Both hubs can support other FC-AL devices at their physical locations. Stated distances assume a 50 micron multimode cable.

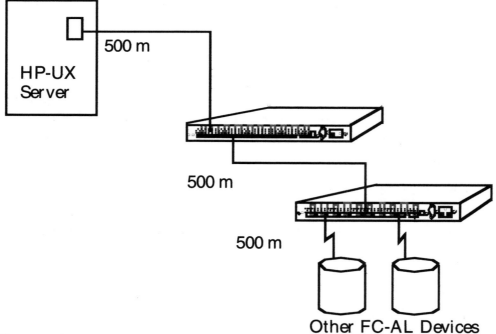

Figure 3-9   Cascaded Shortwave Hub Topology

3.4.2 Cascading Long-wave Hubs

Cascaded FC-AL, non-OFC, long-wave hubs use the long-wave port for the hub-to-hub connection. Ports 1 through 9 on each long-wave hub are for connections to FC-AL devices. When cascading long-wave hubs, only use the long-wave port on each hub to connect the hubs. The overall distance in this topology is 11,000 meters. There is 500m from the server to the first hub, plus 10,000m between the two long-wave hubs, plus 500m from the second hub to the final device.

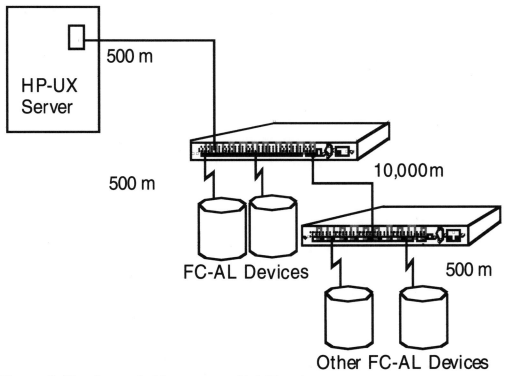

Figure 3-10   Cascaded Long-wave Hub Topology

Addressing

This chapter discusses:

- **The addressing limitations of HP-UX**
- **Work-arounds**
- **Three methods of addressing**
    - **Peripheral Device addressing**
    - **Logical Unit addressing**
    - **Volume Set addressing**
- **Reading Hardware paths**

4.1 The Addressing Limitations of HP-UX

As discussed in the previous chapter, Fibre Channel allows a potentially very large number of available addresses. However, this large number of available addresses does not fit seamlessly into the current addressing model in the HP-UX operating system. To handle the number of possible addresses, the Fibre Channel Protocol (FCP) subsystem on HP-UX uses three methods of addressing:

• Peripheral Device addressing

• Logical Unit addressing

• Volume Set addressing

But first, there are two major limitations and work-arounds that need to be explained.

4.1.1 Target Address Space Limitations

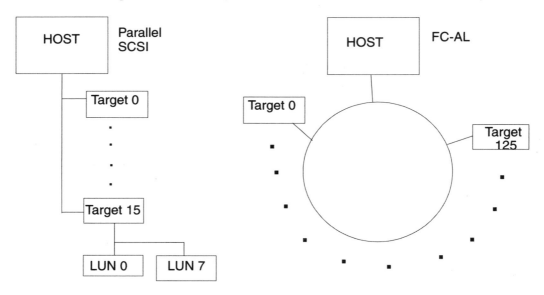

Figure 4-1   Target Address Space Limitations

Parallel SCSI has the capacity to handle 16 IDs (targets or devices) per bus, 15 devices and one controller. The controller is the HBA. FC-AL, however, has a much larger potential number of targets that can be addressed, 0–125 or 126 devices.

4.1.2 LUN Address Space Limitations

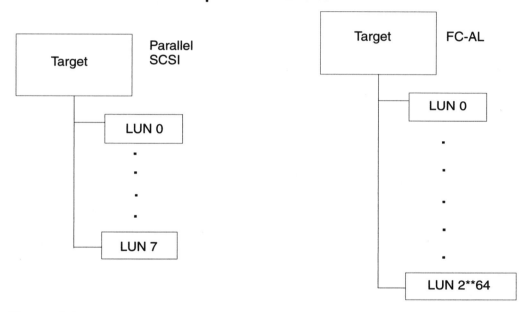

Figure 4-2 LUN Address Space Limitations

Parallel SCSI has the capacity to handle eight LUNs per target or device. FC-AL, however has a huge potential number of LUNs: 2^{64}.

4.1.3 Work-arounds for Target Address Space Limitations

In order to address the 126 targets allowed by FC-AL, HP-UX incoporates the use of virtual busses. Each virtual bus addresses a group of 16 FC-AL targets.

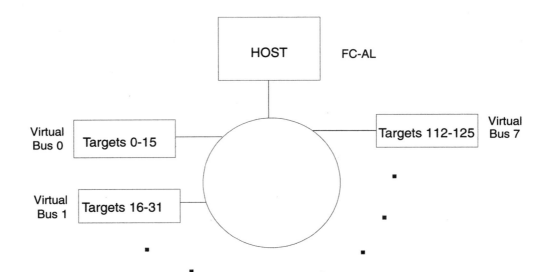

Figure 4-3   Work-around for Target Address Limitations

4.1.4   Work-around for LUN Address Space Limitations

In order to address all the allowable LUNs, HP-UX enables 128 LUNs per virtual bus.

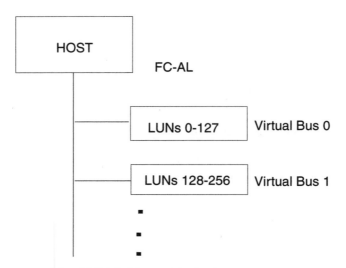

Figure 4-4   Work-around for LUN Address Limitations

4.2 Addressing Methods for HP-UX

As mentioned previously, there are three methods used by HP-UX for Fibre Channel addressing in order to work around the HP-UX limitations[1].

- Peripheral Device addressing
- Logical Unit addressing
- Volume Set addressing

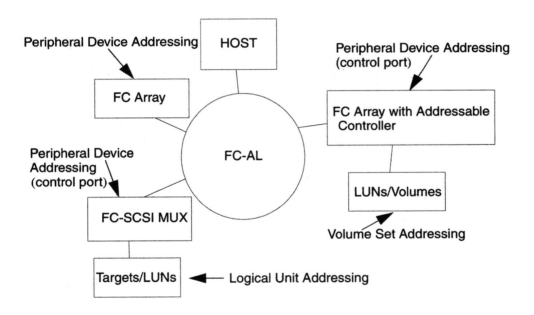

Figure 4-5   Addressing Methods

The Fibre Channel Protocol (FCP) has a very large address space mapped onto the parallel SCSI address model of HP-UX. The FCP portion of the SCSI subsystem on HP-UX handles the large target address space associated with Fibre Channel by creating multiple virtual SCSI buses.

1.   These limitations will be resolved with a new version of HP-UX, soon to be released.

The FCP LUN ID is 8 bytes in length. All LUN addressing is done in the first two bytes. The control port of a device with an addressable controller uses Peripheral Device addressing.

Hewlett-Packard's 30-slot Fibre Channel disk array is not a true array. It does not have an addressable control port. Each LUN is addressed as though it were directly attached.

4.2.1 Hardware Path for Fibre Channel Addressing

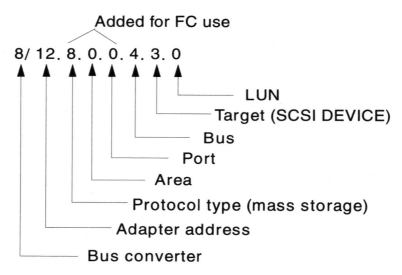

Figure 4-6   Hardware Path

Addressing begins as it would on any Hewlett-Packard computer system. The Bus converter and HBA addresses have the same format and meanings as on all previous Hewlett-Packard products. However, the protocol type, area and port have been added for use with Fibre Channel. The protocol type is "8" for mass storage and "5" for networking. For Fibre Channel mass storage devices, the protocol type will always be "8."

The Area is always "0" for private loop. The Port is not always "0" and will be covered in following pages.

The HBA takes the highest soft address on the loop. This address does not show up in the hardware path. A soft address is an address used if there are duplicate hard addresses on a loop. Devices on a loop must not be allowed to acquire a soft address because of the possibility that a device could acquire a different soft address if power fails for a device on a loop and later is restored. For more information refer to the section "Hard versus Soft addresses" at the end of this chapter.

A Hewlett-Packard FC-AL hub does not have a Fibre Channel address and is therefore not seen in an ioscan output. The hub is a pass-through device that increases reliability by electrically bypassing nodes that are causing problems on the loop and has no loop address of its own.

4.2.2 Peripheral Device Addressing

This addressing method is used for addressing the FC-SCSI MUX (discussed in Chapter 5), controller, and certain other Fibre Channel array controllers. The Hewlett-Packard High-Availability Fibre Channel Disk Array (HA FC Disk Array) also uses this type of addressing for its controller. This type of addressing is also used for targets with eight or fewer LUNs.

Peripheral device addressing is used with devices that do not specify a device type of array controller for LUN0 and do not use Logical Unit addressing or Volume Set addressing. This addressing method is specified by the Private Loop Device Attach profile standard. Although the profile is an 8-bit LUN field HP-UX limits the address to values 0 through 7.

4.2.2.1 Loop Addressing in ioscan

The HA FC disk array uses Peripheral Device addressing exclusively. The loop address for this device must be set physically. There are switches on the controllers that accomplish this. These switches are set in hexadecimal values. The hardware path displays this address as two separate fields (called nibbles, they are half a byte each) in decimal.

For example, the loop address is set by using the device switches, located on the controller face-plate. These switches have hexadecimal values. For this example the switches are set at 3C. The decimal value is then derived by separating the two characters, converting from HEX, and then separating them with a period. See Figure 4-7.

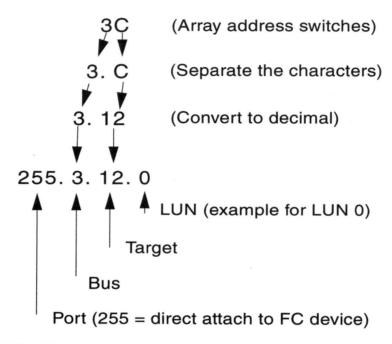

Figure 4-7   Nibble Conversion of Loop Address on a 30-Slot Array

The hardware path for the device shows each nibble as a decimal value separated by a period.

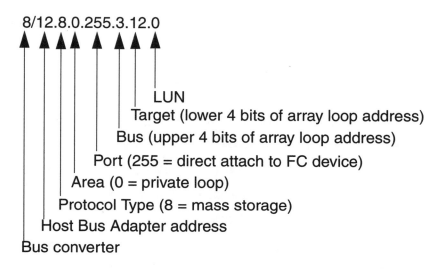

Figure 4-8 Example of LUN using Peripheral Device Addressing

This example shows LUN 0 with a loop address of decimal 60. The Loop address is represented in the Bus and Target fields. The HEX 3C is converted to a decimal 60.

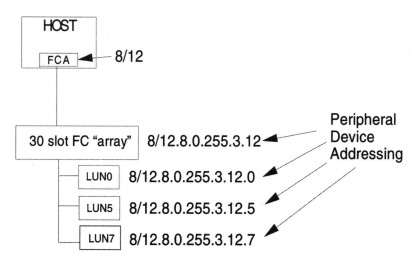

Figure 4-9 Hewlett-Packard HA FC Disk Array

In this example, LUN 0 is an addressable device and not the control port. The Hewlett-Packard HA FC Disk Array uses Peripheral Device addressing exclusively.

Figure 4-10 is an example ioscan for a disk array.

```
Class    I  H/W Path          Driver  S/W State  H/W Type   Description

=================================================================================

fcp      0  8/12.8            fcp     CLAIMED    INTERFACE  FCP Protocol Adapter

ext_bus 10  8/12.8.0.255.3    fcpdev  CLAIMED    INTERFACE  FCP Device Interface

target   8  8/12.8.0.255.3.12 tgt     CLAIMED    DEVICE

disk    76  8/12.8.0.255.3.12.1 sdisk CLAIMED    DEVICE     DGC C3400WDR5

disk    77  8/12.8.0.255.3.12.2 sdisk CLAIMED    DEVICE     DGC C3400WDR5
```

Figure 4-10   Example of an ioscan

4.2.2.2   Loop Addressing in Grid Manager

When using the Hewlett-Packard HA FC Disk Array remember the Loop ID must be set using the switches in the back of the unit located on the controllers. In our examples the Loop ID of 3C is used. When displaying this in Grid Manager, is shows up as the decimal number 60. This conversion uses the normal HEX to decimal conversion.

If the switches are set to something other than 3C, remember to make the conversion from HEX to decimal. For example, if the switches are set to 2C, then the HEX conversion will be 44 in decimal.

4.2.3 Logical Unit Addressing

This addressing method is used for addressing the SCSI devices attached to the FC-SCSI MUX. Remember, the MUX itself uses Peripheral Device addressing. It has an addressable control port, however, the devices attached to the MUX will use Logical Unit addressing.

HP-UX selects the Logical Unit addressing method based on inquiry data and LUN information returned by the REPORT LUNS command. HP-UX limits the target addresses to addresses 0 through 15 and LUN addresses 0 through 7. The address specifies a bus number (3 bits), a target number (6 bits), and a LUN (5 bits).

Each SCSI bus on the MUX is represented by a separate virtual bus on HP-UX. The MUX control port resides on a different virtual bus than its attached devices. See Figure 4-11 for an example.

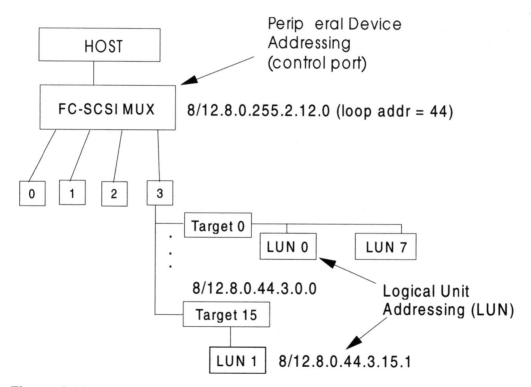

Figure 4-11   Example of Logical Unit Addressing

What this figure shows is the MUX has its own address (8/12.8.0.255.2.12.0), with a loop address of HEX 2C or decimal 44, using Peripheral Device Addressing.

While on virtual SCSI bus 3, target 0, LUN 0 has it's own address (8/12.8.0.44.3.0.0), and LUN 1 of target 15 has its own address, (8/12.8.0.44.3.15.1) using Logical Unit Addressing.

4.2.3.1 Deriving the MUX loop address

The Port field from the path of a device attached to the MUX is first translated into HEX. Next, the HEX numbers are separated into the Bus and Target fields, and, finally, the numbers are converted back to decimal. See Figure 4-12 for the example.

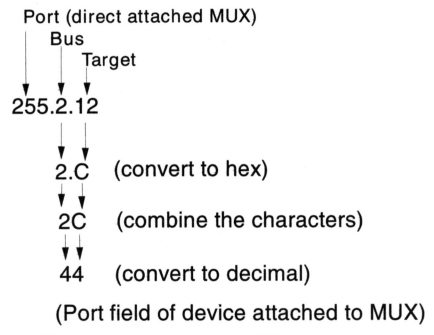

Figure 4-12   Example for Converting the MUX Loop Address

This procedure for conversion is primarily used during troubleshooting to determine the hard address of the MUX.

The next example shows the hardware path of the FC-SCSI MUX control port. The value of 255 in the Bus field indicates that the MUX control port uses the Peripheral Device addressing method and is directly connected to an FC device. Compare with Figure 4-11.

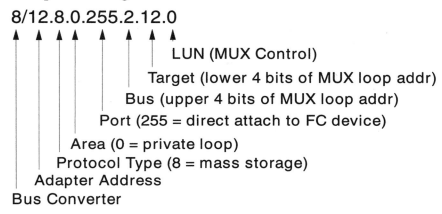

Figure 4-13   Hardware Path for the MUX Control Port

The next example shows the resulting hardware path for a device attached to SCSI bus 3 on the MUX. Again, compare with Figure 4-11.

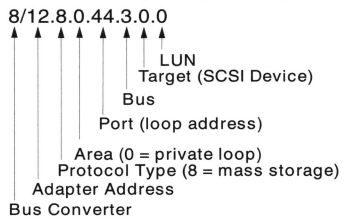

Figure 4-14   Example Hardware Path for a Device on MUX bus 3

The Bus field in the LUN hardware path is the SCSI bus number on the MUX. The Port field in the LUN hardware path is the loop address in decimal.

The hardware path for the MUX control port contains the loop address in the Bus and Target fields.

```
#ioscan -fn

Class    I   H/W Path           Driver    S/W State  H/W Type   Description
=================================================================================
fcp      0   8/8.8              fcp       CLAIMED    INTERFACE  FCP Protocol Adapter
ext_bus  12  8/8.8.0.44.0       fcpmux    CLAIMED    INTERFACE  HP A3308 FCP-SCSI MUX Interface
target   17  8/8.8.0.44.0.4     tgt       CLAIMED    DEVICE
tape     1   8/8.8.0.44.0.4.0   stape     CLAIMED    DEVICE     Quantum DLT4000
                                /dev/rmt/1m          /dev/rmt/c12t4d0BEST
                                /dev/rmt/1mb         /dev/rmt/c12t4d0BESTb
                                /dev/rmt/1mn         /dev/rmt/c12t4d0BESTn
                                /dev/rmt/1mmb        /dev/rmt/c12t4d0BESTnb


                .
                .
                .

ext_bus  16  8/8.8.0.255.2      fcpdev    CLAIMED    INTERFACE  FCP Device Interface
target   28  8/8.8.0.255.2.12   tgt       CLAIMED    DEVICE
ctl      12  8/8.8.0.255.2.12.0 sctl      CLAIMED    DEVICE     HP HPA3308
```

Figure 4-15   Example MUX ioscan with Attached Devices

4.2.4 Volume Set Addressing

This addressing method is used primarily for addressing virtual busses, targets, and LUNs. The HP-UX operating system selects the Volume Set addressing method based on inquiry data and LUN information returned by the SCSI-3 REPORT LUNs command.

A 14-bit volume number supports up to 16,384 LUNs for a single FCP target:

- bits 13–7 become the bus in the hardware path
- bits 6–3 become the target in the hardware path
- bits 2–0 become the LUN in the hardware path

For example, in Volume Set addressing, the control port of a Fibre Channel Disk Array uses Peripheral Device addressing and the LUNs (also known as volumes) will use Volume Set addressing.

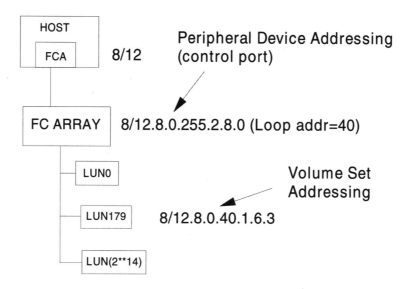

Figure 4-16 Example of Volume Set Addressing

What Figure 4-16 shows is that the FC disk array has a peripheral device address of 8/12.8.0.255.2.8.0 and LUN number 179 has a volume set address of 8/12.8.0.40.1.6.3. The address of the LUN number incorporates the loop address number of 40. The following sections describe how to interrupt this addressing scheme.

4.2.4.1   Deriving the Volume Set Address

Using the example in Figure 4-16, for LUN number 179 the following conversion can be done.

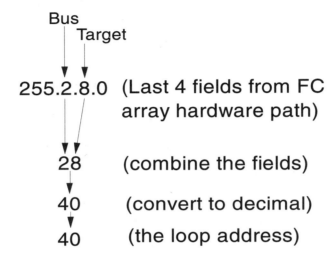

Bus
    Target

255.2.8.0 (Last 4 fields from FC
               array hardware path)

28   (combine the fields)

40   (convert to decimal)

40   (the loop address)

Figure 4-17   Example of Deriving Loop Address using Volume Set Addressing

The bus and target fields are used in the hardware path of the Fibre Channel array controller to represent the loop address. Also remember that all hardware paths with Port=255 use the Peripheral Devices addressing method. Also, in this example the zero at the end of the string represents the LUN number.

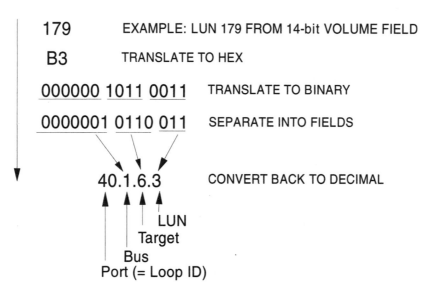

Figure 4-18 Deriving a LUN Hardware Path

Again using the example in Figure 4-16, the following conversion takes place.

If a calculator is not available to perform the hexadecimal or binary conversions, divide the decimal value by 16 and convert the result to hexadecimal. Then convert the remainder to hexadecimal. For our example, refer to Figure 4-16, the ioscan for LUN 179 would shows as follows.

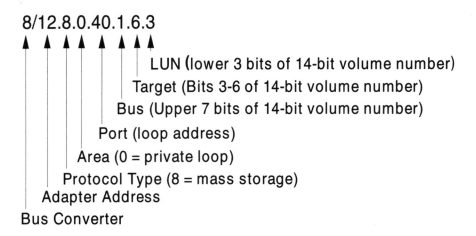

Figure 4-19   Final Hardware Path for LUN 179

4.2.5 Hard versus Soft Addresses

The FC-AL protocol allows for soft addresses to be assigned to devices if duplicate hard addresses are found on the loop. However, it is best to avoid allowing devices to acquire a soft address. The only way to avoid allowing devices to acquire a soft address is to make sure that all devices have unique hard addresses before they are attached to the loop.

Create a loop map and verify that any device added has a different hard address than devices already on the loop. It really is worth repeating, *Make sure all devices attached to the loop have a unique hard address.* Always run an ioscan after attaching a device to confirm that the device obtained its hard address.

For example, one array with address 3C attached to an FCA poses no problem. And two arrays, each with address 3C, attached to two FCAs pose no problem. However, two arrays, each with address 3C, attached to a hub will pose a problem. One will have a hard address and the other will be assigned a soft address. The first array to acquire the loop will receive its hard address and the second array will be assigned a soft address because the loop will see a duplicate hard address.

After a disconnect or a power off condition, the loop may initialize with "flip-flopped" addresses. This can produce data corruption. Upon power on the array that had the soft address may acquire the loop first and receive its hard address and the array that had the hard address before the power off condition now will be assigned a soft address. The data stored on that device when it had a hard address is no longer accessible or even know to the system because of the address "flip-flop."

To prevent this condition assign each device a unique hard address.

Hewlett-Packard Fibre Channel Products

This chapter discusses:

- **Hewlett-Packard Fibre Channel products** [1]
  - **Two of Hewlett-Packard's Fibre Channel Chips**
  - **Fibre Channel Adapters**
  - **FC-AL Hub**
  - **High Availability Fibre Channel Disk Array**
  - **SCSI Multiplexer**
  - **Hewlett-Packard's Fibre Channel Switch**
- **Hewlett-Packard systems supporting Fibre Channel** [2]
- **Topologies/solutions using Fibre Channel**

1. Hewlett-Packard will be producing new/more products as time goes on.

2. Hewlett-Packard will be adding more systems to the supported list as they become available.

5.1 CONTROLLER IC's

5.1.1 Overview

Hewlett-Packard began shipping the TACHYON IC in early 1995 and today, TACHYON is the industry's leading Fibre Channel controller. HP has carried this leadership forward with the Tachyon TL IC, a 64-bit PCI-to-Fibre Channel controller, that focuses on arbritrated loop topologies for cost-effective, Fibre Channel mass storage designs. Both of these IC's implement the TACHYON family architecture, which is a complete hardware-based design that delivers on the true performance capabilities of Fibre Channel.

5.1.2 TACHYON

Controller IC

HPFC-5000C

The Industry's Leading Fibre Channel Controller IC

5.1.2.1 Product Highlights

• Single chip Fibre Channel interface

• Supports both networking and mass storage implementations

• Complete hardware-based design uniquely optimized for Fibre Channel performance

• Released to production June 1996

5.1.2.2 Description

The TACHYON controller IC, HPFC-5000C, supports Arbitrated Loop, fabric, and point-to-point topologies; Class 1, 2 and 3 services; and supports quarter, half, and full-speed Fibre Channel data rates. The IC also provides on-chip support of FCP for SCSI initiators and targets and hardware assists for TCP/UDP/IP networking. Performance is optimized within the IC through complete concurrency with eight internal DMA channels and full duplex processing.

The TACHYON IC is unique in the industry with its level of maturity, interoperability, and broad design-in activity. First released by HP to customers for development in early 1995, the TACHYON IC is currently designed-in by more than 30 OEMs and has become the defacto controller IC choice for Fibre Channel.

* Special conditions apply regarding the sale of the TACHYON IC. Contact your local HP Components Sales Representative for details.

Figure 5-1   Hewlett-Packard's Fibre Channel Chips

5.1.3 TACHYON TL Fibre Channel Arbitrated Loop Controller

HPFC-5100 (For more information, send an email with your address and telephone number to hsio@hp.com.)

5.1.3.1   Features

- Second generation controller IC, based on HP's TACHYON architecture
- Targeted to Fibre Channel Arbitrated Loop (FC-AL) designs, including Public Loop Support
- Supports both Class 2 and 3
- 1 Gigabit/second Fibre Channel rate
- Full Duplex support with parallel inbound and outbound processing
- 32/64-bit PCI interface, compliant to PCI v2.1
- Complete hardware handling of entire SCSI I/O via FCP on-chip assists
- Full Initiator and Target mode functionality

5.1.3.2 Description

The HPFC-5100, Tachyon TL, is a second-generation controller that leverages HP's extensive experience in Fibre Channel, established with the original TACHYON controller. Tachyon TL carries forward the assurance of interoperability and true Fibre Channel performance. Tachyon TL focuses on mass storage applications that require FC-AL, Class 3 and 2 (ACK0), and SCSI upper layer protocol handling. Coupled with a high performance 32/64-bit PCI bus interface, Tachyon TL provides a cost-effective, high performance mass storage solution.

Tachyon TL continues with the TACHYON architecture, a complete hardware-based state machine design. This architecture avoids on-chip microprocessor performance issues of a single processing resource, processor cycles per second, and access times to firmware. Rather, the TACHYON architecture is designed to realize the full potential of Fibre Channel. Tachyon TL provides the highest levels of concurrency by way of numerous independent functional blocks providing parallel processing of data, control and commands. In addition, these blocks process at hardware speeds versus firmware speeds and automate the entire SCSI I/O in hardware. The result is minimized latency and I/O overhead, coupled with the highest levels of parallelism to provide maximum I/O rates and bandwidth.

5.1.3.3 FC-AL Features

In addition to the high performance architecture, Tachyon TL offers second generation Fibre Channel features, such as Public Loop, Auto Status, multiple I/O's in the same loop arbitration cycle, loop map, loop broadcast, and loop directed reset. These features allow the designer to achieve higher performance in an arbitrated loop topology.

5.1.3.4   Physical Layer

The physical layer interface is the popular 10-bit wide specification that allows interfacing to a low-cost serializer/deserializer (SerDes) IC. This is the same physical layer interface that is popular on Fibre Channel disk drives today due to its quality gigabit signaling, small form factor, and low-cost.

5.1.3.5   Applications

- Motherboard integration
- Host Bus Adapters
- Storage Subsystems
- I2O designs

5.1.4 TACHYON Block Diagrams

TACHYON is a fundamental building block compatible with Hewlett-Packard's Fibre Channel solution which includes interface controllers, physical link modules, adapters, switches, and disk drives.

The TACHYON architecture supports both networking and mass storage connections to provide a low cost, high performance solution with low host overhead.

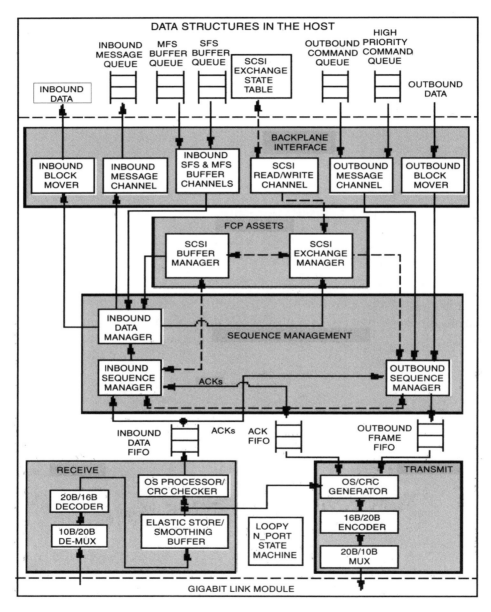

Figure 5-2   TACHYON Internal Block Diagram

5.1.4.1   Features

- Single chip Fibre Channel intercace (no I/O processor required)
- Supports 1062.5, 531, and 266 MBaud links
- Supports three topologies; direct connect, fabric, and Fibre Channel Arbitrated Loop (FC-AL)
- Supports Fibre Channel Class 1,2, and 3 Services
- Supports up to 2-Kbyte frame payload for all classes of service
- Sequence segmentation/reassembly in hardware
- Automatic ACK frame generation and processing
- On-chip support of FCP for SCSI Initiators and Targets
- Supports up to 16,384 concurrent SCSI I/O transactions
- Compliant with Interned MIB-II network management
- Direct interface to industry standard 10 and 20-bit Gigabit Link Modules (GLM)
- Hardware assists for TCP/UDP/IP networking
- Parity protectin on internal data path
- Eight internal DMA channels
- Full duplex internal architecture that allows TACHYON to process inbound and outbound data simultaneously

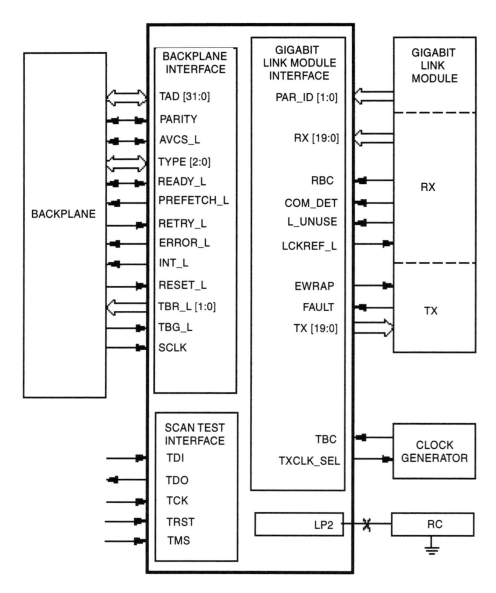

Figure 5-3   TACHYON Pin-out Block Diagram

5.1.4.2 Specifications

- System Clock Frequency:
  - 24–40 MHz backplane operation

- Operating Temperature:
  - 0–50 degrees C @ 0 m/s airflow
  - 0–70 degrees C @ 1.5 m/s airflow

- Testability:
  - Full internal scan path
  - IEEE standard 1149.1 Boundary Scan

- Packaging:
  - 208-pin metal quad flat pack

- Standards:
  - Intended to be compliant with ANSI standards and FCSI/FCA profile defintions

5.1.4.3 Product Disclaimer

HP reserves the right to alter specifications, features, capabilities, functions, and even general availability of the product at any time. Special conditions apply regarding the sale of the Tachyon TL IC; For more information, send an email with your address and telephone number to hsio@hp.com.

5.2 Fibre Channel Adapter for the K-Class Systems

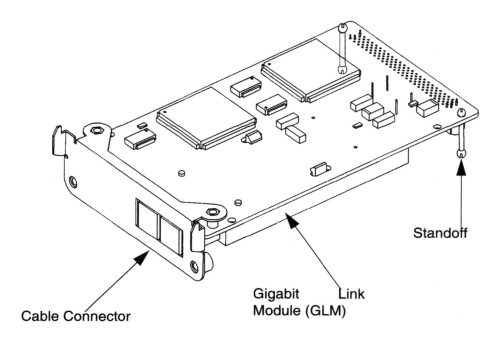

Standoff

Cable Connector

Gigabit   Link
Module (GLM)

Figure 5-4   A3404A Fibre Channel Adapter (for K-Class Systems)

This Fibre Channel Adapter (FCA) is designed for K-Class systems, models K2xx, K3xx, K4xx, and K5xx. It is a full speed (1063 Mbps), shortwave, non-OFC device.

Although it is similar to the product used for T-Class systems, this adapter has a different bulkhead and standoffs near the rear connector for shock and vibration protection. It cannot be interchanged with T-Class–type adapters.

5.3 Fibre Channel Adapter for the T-Class Systems

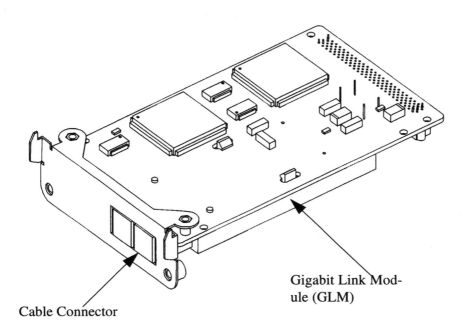

Gigabit Link Module (GLM)

Cable Connector

Figure 5-5   A3636A Fibre Channel Adapter (for T-Class Systems)

This FCA is designed for T-Class systems, model T600. It is a full speed (1063 Mbps), shortwave, non-OFC device.

Although it is similar to the product used for the K-Class systems, this adapter has a different bulkhead and no standoffs near the rear connector. It cannot be interchanged with K-Class–type adapters.

5.4 Fibre Channel Adapter for the D-Class Systems

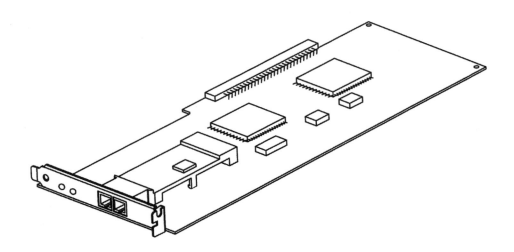

Figure 5-6   A3591A Fibre Channel Adapter (for D-Class Systems)

This Fibre Channel Adapter (FCA) is designed for D-Class systems. It is a full speed (1063 Mbps), shortwave, non-OFC device.

5.5 Fibre Channel Adapter for the V-Class Systems

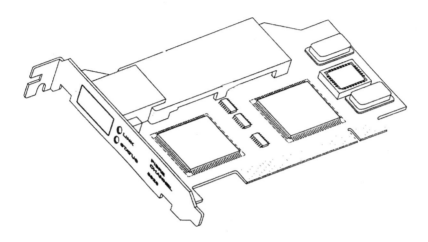

Figure 5-7   A3740A Fibre Channel Adapter (for V-Class Systems)

This Fibre Channel Adapter (FCA) is designed for V-Class systems. It is a full speed (1063 Mbps), shortwave, non-OFC device.

5.6 Fibre Channel Arbitrated Loop Hub

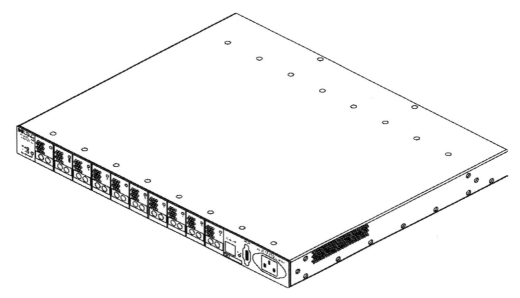

Figure 5-8   A3724A/A4839A FC-AL Hub

The FC-AL hub is available in shortwave and long-wave models. Both models are available in stand-alone or factory-racked configurations. The AZ models are the factory-racked models.

5.6.1 Features

• The shortwave hub has ten non-OFC shortwave optical transceivers.

• The long-wave hub has nine non-OFC, shortwave optical transceivers and one non-OFC, long-wave optical transceiver.

• Local retime and regeneration of transmit signals to prevent accumulation of jitter and improve the signal.

• Reliable, automatic bypass of failed nodes; dynamic recognition of newly added or removed nodes, with a controller in each port permitting the bypass of a port if the port fails signal validity tests.

- Active loop reconfiguration when a node to an arbitrated loop is added, removed, or moved.

- Plug-and-play capability, allowing the hub to connect to compatible servers and other FC-AL devices while they are operating. FC-AL devices can be added or removed while the hub is active.

5.6.2 Shortwave Hub (HP A3724A/AZ)

The short-wave hub supports 10 non-OFC (non-open fiber control) shortwave FC-AL connections. In arbitrated loop topology, the data rates and wavelength between ports must be the same. The shortwave hub supports only gigabit shortwave to gigabit shortwave connections using fiber cables.

For the shortwave hub, Hewlett-Packard recommends 50 micron multimode fiber cable for new installations but supports 62.5 micron multimode fiber cable with SC-style connectors in existing installations. Installations can mix 50 micron and 62.5 micron cables.

Using a 50 micron multimode cable, the short-wave hub supports distances up to 500 meters between a server host and the hub, between a hub port and a connected FC-AL device, and between two hubs. The maximum distance between a host server and FC-AL devices connected to cascaded shortwave hubs is 1500 meters.

5.6.3 Long-wave Hub (HP A4839A/AZ)

The long-wave hub supports nine non-OFC, shortwave devices and a second long-wave FC-AL hub. The long-wave hub supports shortwave gigabit to shortwave gigabit connections from ports 1 through 9 using fiber cables. The long-wave hub also supports a long-wave hub to long-wave hub connection from the long-wave port.

For the long-wave port, Hewlett-Packard recommends 9 micron multimode fiber cable. For ports 1 through 9, Hewlett-Packard recommends 50 micron multimode fiber cable for new installations but supports 62.5 micron multimode fiber cable with SC-style connectors in existing installations.

For ports 1 through 9, the long-wave hub supports distances of 500 meters between the port and a connected FC-AL device. For the long-wave port, the long-wave hub supports distances up to 10 kilometers between two long-wave hubs.

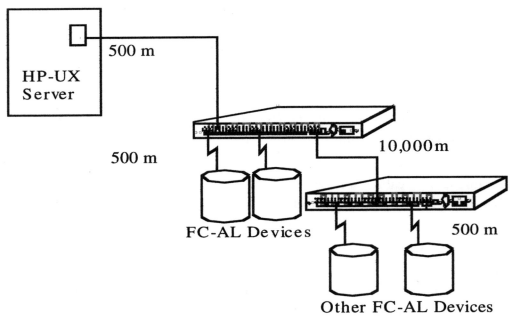

Figure 5-9   Cascaded Long-wave   Hub Topology

5.6.4 Plan the FC-AL Connections

The hub does not require drivers or specific versions of the HP-UX operating system, but FC-AL devices that connect to the hub do. Contact an HP sales representative for information on hardware and software requirements for the FC-AL devices you plan to connect to the hub.

1. Verify the loop cabling configuration is correct by comparing it to the cabling examples in Section 5.6.4.1. Modify the network cabling map as needed.

   Note: Incorrect wiring can lead to problems such as devices left off the loop and inaccessible by the server. Follow the guidelines below before starting.

2. Review the user-assigned loop ID (hardware address) of every FC-AL device to be connected to the hub and make sure that each ID is unique. Duplicate IDs on the loop can cause problems. In addition, each device has its own factory-assigned unique worldwide name.

3. Verify the connections between the hub port and the FC-AL mass storage device or the FC-AL adapter are of the same wave type and speed. For example, plan to connect a port on the hub to a shortwave FC-AL device.

4. Document the planned connections in a cabling map if not already done.

5.6.4.1   Correct Cabling Examples

In a cascaded configuration, connect any port on the first hub to any port on the second hub. The following example includes all 18 nodes in the loop formed by FC-AL Device 1, Hub A, Hub B, and FC-AL Device 2. FC-AL Device 1 is connected to Port 1 on Hub A; Port 10 of Hub A connects to Port 1 of Hub B, and Port 10 on Hub B connects to FC-AL Device 2. In this configuration, Port 10 on Hub B can connect to any FC-AL device. This is just one example of cascaded hubs. The connection between hubs can occupy any combination of ports.

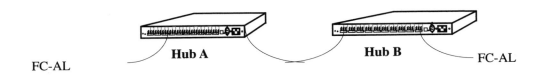

FC-AL

Hub A

Hub B

FC-AL

Figure 5-10   Cascaded Shortwave FC-AL Hub Configuration

5.6.4.2   Incorrect Cabling Examples

The following illustrations are examples of incorrect cabling. For example: Do NOT cable together two ports on the same hub. Ports between the two connections will be eliminated from the loop.

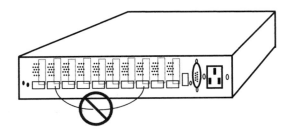

Figure 5-11   Incorrect Cabling Example: Connected Ports on the Same Hub

Do NOT attach more than one cable between any two hubs.

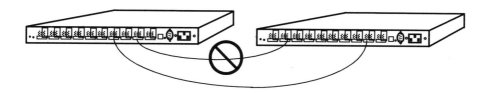

Figure 5-12 Incorrect cabling example: more than one cable connection between hubs

Do NOT attempt to connect a hub to more than one other hub.

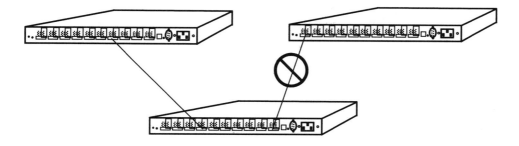

Figure 5-13 Incorrect cabling example: more than two hubs connected

5.7 High Availability Fibre Channel Disk Array

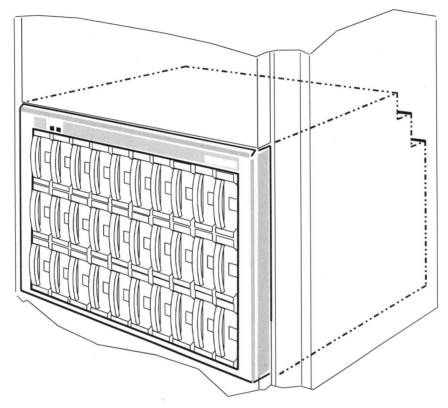

Figure 5-14   A3661A HA FC Disk Array

This Fibre Channel peripheral has substantial storage capacity. It will hold up to 30 disk modules. Hewlett-Packard's highest capacity point is 18 gigabytes per disk module. This will increase with future releases. This disk array was designed specifically for use in Fibre Channel topologies.

It is High Availability (HA) because it employs redundant components such as:

- disk modules
- power supplies
- controller units

It is supported by the K-, D-, T- (600 only), and V-Class Hewlett-Packard Enterprise Servers running HP-UX 10.20 TFC or later. It has 1.063 gigabit per second optical Fibre Channel link speed and Fibre Channel Arbitrated Loop (FC-AL) topology is also supported.

5.7.1 Basic Topology

The disk array protects against single points of failure with RAID (Redundant Array of Independent Disks) technology, global hot spares, and redundant, hot-swappable, customer-replaceable disk array components. Many of the components can be removed and replaced by the customer while the disk array is powered up, without removing it from the cabinet and without losing data. The RAID levels supported are 5, 3, 1/0, and 1. RAID level 0 and individual disk units are not supported because they provide no data redundancy.

Disk arrays and hosts can be directly or indirectly connected to Hewlett-Packard FC-AL Hubs in a number of hardware topologies.

Figure 5-15 shows the high availability version of the basic topology implemented on a host system with two host FC I/O adapters connected to a dual-SP disk array.

Basic Topology

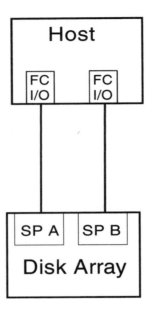

Figure 5-15   Basic Topology, High Availability Version: Host with Two FC I/O Adapters

One high availability version of the basic topology can be implemented in D-Class servers.

Basic Topology

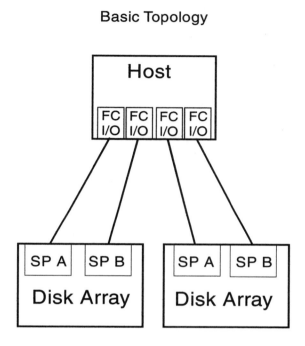

Figure 5-16   Basic Topology, High Availability Version: Host with Four FC I/O
Adapters

Figure 5-16 shows the high availability version of the basic topology
implemented on a host with four host FC I/O adapters. Two of the FC adapters
are connected to one dual-SP disk array while the other two FC adapters are
connected to a second dual-SP disk array. Each connection of host adapter and
SP creates a separate FC-AL. Additional disk arrays and FC adapters can be
installed in T-Class servers.

The nonhigh availability version connects a host or server to one or more
single-SP disk arrays. This version provides no hardware redundancy and does
not protect against single points of SP, FC cable, host FC I/O adapter, or internal
SCSI-2 bus failure. If any of these components fail, the disk array becomes
unavailable and applications cannot continue to run. The disk array remains
unavailable until the failed hardware component is replaced. Applications can
continue to run after the failure of single disk modules within logical disk units
(LUNs).

Figure 5-17 shows the nonhigh availability version of the basic topology implemented on either a K-Class or T-Class with four FC I/O adapters connected to single SPs in four disk Each connection between adapter and SP creates a separate FC-AL. Additional disk arrays and FC adapters can be installed in T-Class servers.

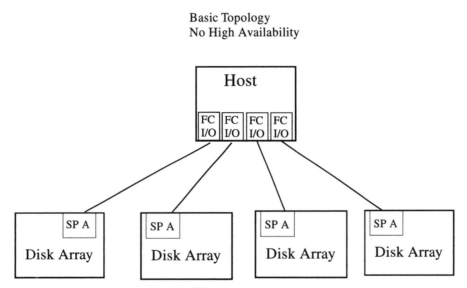

Basic Topology
No High Availability

Figure 5-17   Basic Topology, NonHigh Availability Version: Host with Four FC I/O Adapters

All the topologies covered up to this point are considered to be basic topologies and are limited in distance to 500 meters because they do not incorporate the use of a hub. Using a hub in the topology can increase the distance the Fibre Channel peripheral can be placed from the host, but remember it will also increase the complexity of the topology.

The following figures will demonstrate the use of hubs in topologies when just connecting to disk arrays.The use of hubs not only increases distance but also the degree of high availability and storage capacity available to the host(s).

Each instance of the single-system distance topology generally uses the following hardware components:

- One host system or server

- Two FC I/O adapters

- One 10-port HP FC-AL Hub (A3724A)

- One to four dual-SP disk arrays (for high availability) or one to eight single-SP disk arrays (for nonhigh availability)

- Maximum 500 m fibre optic cable distance on each connection between the host and the HP FC-AL Hub and between the HP FC-AL Hub and each disk array, for a total FC-AL cable length not to exceed 5000 m

One or two single-distance topologies can be implemented in D-Class and K-Class systems, and up to 11 instances of this topology can be implemented in T-Class servers.

5.7.2 Distance Topology

Figure 5-11 illustrates the single-system distance topology with one host with two FC I/O adapters and three dual-SP disk arrays. In this example two of the HP FC-AL Hub's ten ports are unused.

This topology uses one 10-port HP FC-AL Hub. The two FC I/O adapters in the single host attach to two ports in the HP FC-AL Hub, providing redundant hardware paths between the host and the HP FC-AL Hub. The SPs of dual or single-SP disk arrays attach to some or all of the remaining eight HP FC-AL Hub ports. This topology creates a single FC-AL that resembles a star topology with the HP FC-AL Hub acting as the central switching element. The 10-port HP FC-AL Hub is inserted between the host and the disk arrays, increasing both the number of arrays (and total disk capacity) that can be connected to a single host and the total length of the FC cabling. The HP FC-AL Hub is a single point of failure in this topology.

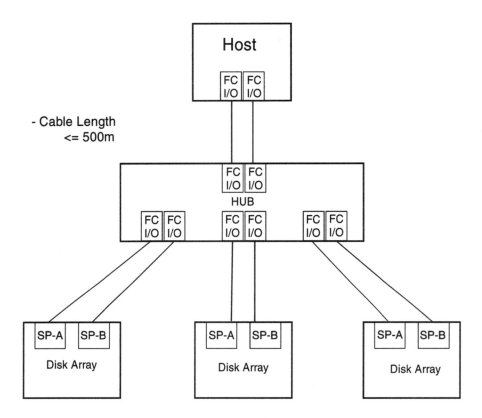

Figure 5-18   Single-System Distance Topology

Supported cable lengths for each segment of the FC-AL include 2 m, 16 m, 50 m, 100 m, and 500 m. The maximum combined cable lengths for all segments, that is, the total length of the FC-AL, should not exceed 5000 m because performance can degrade due to propagation delay. Because of this it is recommended that the total cable length of the FC-AL be as short as possible. Fibre optic cables in lengths of 2 m, 16 m, 50 m, and 100 m cables can be ordered from Hewlett-Packard. Fibre optic cables longer than 100 m must be custom-fabricated for each implementation.

Like the basic topology, both high availability versions (two SPs per disk array) and nonhigh availability versions (one SP per disk array) of this topology can be implemented.

For high availability implementations, up to four disk arrays with two SPs per disk array can be connected to the HP FC-AL Hub. For nonhigh availability implementations, up to eight disk arrays with one SP per disk array can be connected to the HP FC-AL Hub.

For high availability, up to four dual-SP disk arrays can be attached to an HP FC-AL Hub. The two FC I/O adapters installed in the host connect to the two remaining HP FC-AL Hub ports. If one SP fails, ownership of its LUNs can transfer automatically to the remaining operational SP through the other FC adapter. If a primary and an alternate path have been configured in LVM, LVM can switch automatically and transparently to the alternate path. Likewise, if one host adapter fails, or if one FC cable from the host to the HP FC-AL Hub or from the HP FC-AL Hub to one of the dual-SP disk array fails, that disk array can still be accessed via the alternate hardware path. The HP FC-AL Hub is a single point of failure in this topology. If the HP FC-AL Hub fails, no communication between the host and any of the disk arrays is possible.

For nonhigh availability, up to eight single-SP disk arrays can be attached to the HP FC-AL Hub. If the single SP or the FC cable between the HP FC-AL Hub and an array fails, no I/O operations are possible between the host and the disk array with the failed SP. If one FC adapter fails in the host, the disk array can still be accessed via the hardware path through the other operational FC adapter. If the HP FC-AL Hub fails, no communication between the host and any disk arrays is possible.

5.7.3 High Availability Topology

The high availability topology increases the availability of the single system distance topology by protecting against single points of HP FC-AL Hub failure with the use of redundant HP FC-AL Hubs. Adding a second HP FC-AL Hub also increases the number of hosts and disk arrays that can be connected to a single FC-AL.

Each instance of the high availability topology uses the following hardware components:

- Two to four host systems or servers
- Two FC I/O adapters per K-Class or T-Class host
  See your Hewlett-Packard support representative for the number of adapters supported in each model of D-class server
- Two 10-port HP FC-AL Hubs (A3724A)
- Two SPs per disk array
- Maximum of six disk arrays in a four-host FC-AL or maximum of eight disk arrays in a two-host FC-AL
- Maximum 500 m fibre optic cable distance on each connection between each host and HP FC-AL Hub and between each HP FC-AL Hub and disk array, for a total FC-AL cable length not to exceed 5000 m

As its name implies, the high availability topology supports only dual-SP disk arrays. Because the objective of this topology is to use redundant hardware components to provide high availability, disk arrays with single SPs are not supported. All hardware components and paths are redundant. If any hardware failure occurs, I/O communication between host and disk array can be completed through another path.

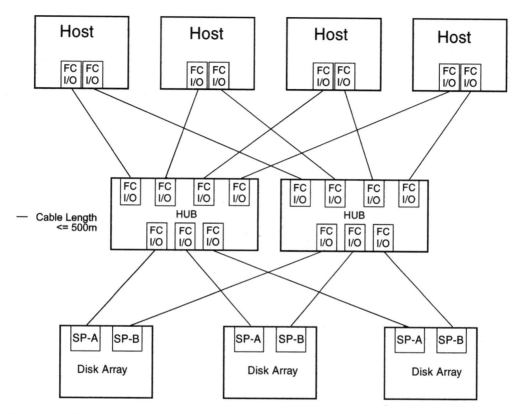

Figure 5-19   High Availability (redundant loop) Topology

In this topology each host uses two FC I/O adapters and each disk array uses dual SPs. One adapter in each host and one SP in each disk array connect to one HP FC-AL Hub, forming one FC-AL. The second adapter in each host and the second SP in each disk array connect to the second HP FC-AL Hub, cabled into a separate FC-AL. This creates two redundant FC-ALs.

Because each HP FC-AL Hub has ten ports, either two hosts and eight disk arrays or four hosts and six disk arrays can attach to each HP FC-AL Hub. If any hardware component (SP, host FC I/O adapter, HP FC-AL Hub, or fibre optic cable) fails in one FC-AL, the I/O communication between hosts and disk arrays can continue through the other FC-AL.

Supported cable lengths for each segment of the FC-AL include 2 m, 16 m, 50 m, 100 m, and 500 m. The maximum combined cable lengths for all segments, that is, the total length of the FC-AL, should not exceed 5000 m because performance can degrade due to propagation delay. Because of this it is recommended that the total cable length of the FC-AL be as short as possible. Fibre optic cables in lengths of 2 m, 16 m, 50 m, and 100 m cables can be ordered from Hewlett-Packard. Fibre optic cables longer than 100 m must be custom-fabricated for each implementation.

5.7.4 High Availability, Distance, and Capacity Topology

The high availability, distance, and capacity topology expands on the high availability topology by using cascaded HP FC-AL Hubs to increase the distance of each FC-AL and the number of devices that can be interconnected on the FC-AL. Cascaded HP FC-AL Hubs are two HP FC-AL Hubs connected together.

Each instance of this topology uses the following hardware components:

• Up to four host systems or servers

• Two FC I/O adapters per host

• Two pairs of cascaded 10-port HP FC-AL Hubs

• Two SPs per disk array

• Maximum of nine dual-SP disk arrays

• Maximum 500 m fibre optic cable distance on each connection between each host and HP FC-AL Hub and between each HP FC-AL Hub and disk array, for a total FC-AL cable length not to exceed 5000 m

Like the high availability topology, this topology supports high availability by using redundant FC-ALs. If a hardware component (FC adapter, HP FC-AL Hub, SP or cables) in one FC-AL fails, I/O communication between hosts and disk arrays can continue through the other FC-AL.

The increased distance is supported by using 10 k fibre optic cable to connect each pair of cascaded HP FC-AL Hubs. If distance is a requirement, it is managed between the two HP FC-AL Hubs. The distance from hosts to HP FC-AL Hubs and from disk arrays to HP FC-AL Hubs should be minimized.

Supported cable lengths for each segment of the FC-AL include 2 m, 16 m, 50 m, 100 m, 500 m, and 10 k. The maximum combined cable lengths for all segments, that is, the total length of the FC-AL, should not exceed 11 k because performance can degrade due to propagation delay.

Because of this it is recommended the total cable length of the FC-AL be as short as possible. Fibre optic cables in lengths of 2 m, 16 m, 50 m, and 100 m cables can be ordered from Hewlett-Packard. Fibre optic cables longer than 100 m must be custom-fabricated for each implementation.

In this configuration a maximum of nine SPs can be attached to an HP FC-AL Hub's tenth port is used to connect to the other HP FC-AL Hub in the cascaded pair, rather than to a host adapter as in the high availability topology.

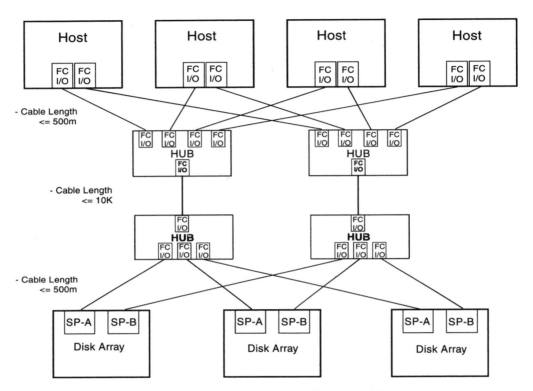

Figure 5-20 High Availability, Distance, and Capacity Topology

5.7.5 Campus Topology

The campus topology uses the same hardware components as the high availability, distance, and capacity topology. The components for each instance of this topology include:

• Up to four host systems or servers

• Two FC I/O adapters per K-Class or T-Class host
(See your Hewlett-Packard support representative for the number of adapters supported in each model of D-class server.)

• Two pairs of cascaded 10-port HP FC-AL Hubs (A3724A)

• Two SPs per disk array

• Maximum of nine disk arrays

• Maximum 500 m fibre optic cable distance on each connection between each host and HP FC-AL Hub and between each HP FC-AL Hub and disk array, for a total FC-AL cable length not to exceed 5000 m

This topology is almost identical to the high availability, distance, and capacity topology. The difference is that in the campus topology one-half of the host systems, HP FC-AL Hubs, and disk arrays are located in one building while the other half of the hosts, HP FC-AL Hubs, and disk arrays are located at another site. The distribution of systems and hardware between two physical sites provides protection against a power failure or some other catastrophic site-wide failure.

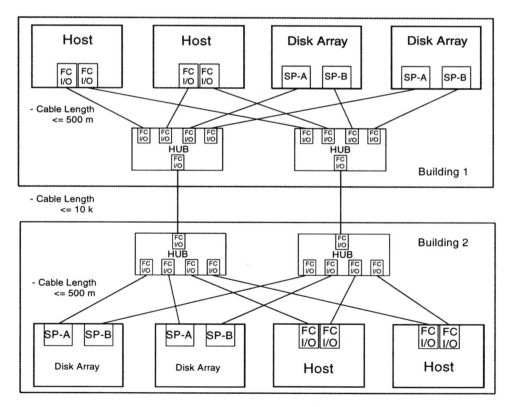

Figure 5-21   Campus Topology

5.8 SCSI Multiplexer

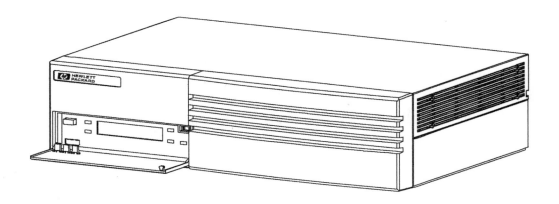

Figure 5-22   A3308A SCSI Multiplexer

Most data centers today are using SCSI technology. Peripheral devices are attached to their host systems through SCSI cables connected to SCSI host bus adapters (HBAs). To use FC technology, however, each system must be able to "speak Fibre Channel." Meeting this requirement usually means expensive purchases and time-consuming conversion, migration of data, and installation of FC-compatible hardware systems and peripherals.

Hewlett-Packard's solution to this concern is the Fibre Channel SCSI Multiplexer (FC-SCSI MUX). The FC-SCSI MUX allows an FC host to use FC technology to transmit data to SCSI type devices. Using the FC-SCSI MUX, customers can extend the distance between a host and peripherals and expand the number of SCSI devices connected to the host.

The MUX multiplexes the inputs and outputs from a single FC connection, HBA, to as many as four SCSI busses. Since each bus can support up to 15 devices, one MUX, theoretically, can support up to 60 devices (with varying levels of performance).

The FC-SCSI MUX permits multiple SCSI mass storage devices to participate in the Fibre Channel architecture. Currently, up to eight SCSI IDs can be
connected through the SCSI MUX and communicate with the host through a
single Fibre Channel link.

The advantage this device affords is to be able to attach existing SCSI
devices to a Fibre Channel mass storage network. Currently Digital Linear Tape
(DLT) libraries are supported, however disk and other SCSI devices will be supported with future releases.

5.8.1 FC-SCSI MUX Topology

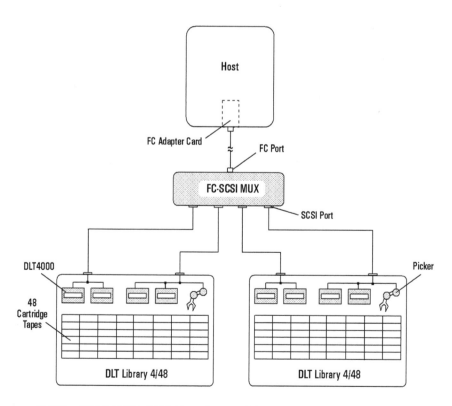

Figure 5-23   FC-SCSI MUX Topology with Two   DLT Libraries

5.9 FC Switch

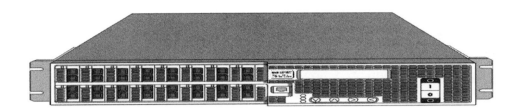

Figure 5-24   Front view of the Hewlett-Packard FC Switch.

Figure 5-25   Back view of the Hewlett-Packard Fibre Channel Switch

The is capable of allowing Fibre Channel connections to either Private Loops (arbitrated loops), or to Fibre Channel Fabric. EPL (Emulated Private Loop), also known as QL (Quick Loop) will be available at first release, and supported on HP-UX 11.0 and HP-UX 10.20 with the appropriate patches. This mode is used to support legacy systems and peripherals previously supported on existing HP-UX 11.0 operating systems. The Fabric support will not be available until the release of HP-UX 11.01, or greater.

The first release will support legacy systems, such as K-Class, D-Class, T-Class, and V-Class, running the above-mentioned HP-UX 10.20 or 11.0 operating system versions. The host systems will use the existing A3404A, A3636A, A3591B, and A3740A Fibre Channel adapters. Once HP-UX 11.01 is available, the FC Switch will be supported using the A5157A dual Tachyon TL Fibre Channel adapter, and the A5158A single Tachyon TL Fibre Channel adapter.

These two new adapters are PCI-based, and will be used in the V2500 and K4000 SPU platforms, on HP-UX 11.01 only.

The Gigabit Fibre Channel Switch will be available in a 16 port configuration (the unit ships with NO GBICs installed), From one to four GBIC options may be used, but at least one must be ordered. Each GBIC option provides four GBICs (GigaBit Interface Converter) which are installed into any desired empty position in the switch. It is possible to use either shortwave, or long-wave GBIC optics. No more than one long wave option may be used at this time.

Use of the long-wave GBIC has limited applications at this time, and any customer wanting to use the long-wave GBIC should request configuration assistance to avoid unsupported/unsupportable configurations which would impair their ability to use this as a SAN (Storage Area Network) solution. The Gigabit Fibre Channel Switch is non-Cascadeable product, meaning only one switch may be used per host connection(s). Multiple hosts may be connected to a single switch.

There is a limit to the number of hosts that can be attached to a single switch. Please reference the Server Configuration Guide on the Hewlett-Packard public Web site at www.hp.com.

The Gigabit Fibre Channel Switch can be use to connect 16 Fibre Channel devices together (consult the Server Configuration Guide for supported configurations). Devices may be either a direct attachment to the switch (as in a Host system, or a Fibre Channel peripheral); or may be through an FC-AL Hub (provides a local loop at that particular attachment); or by way of an FC-SCSI Multiplexer for certain tape or disk configurations (see the Server Configuration Guide).

Only one loop connection may be used per Hub. There is a limit of one loop master per Fabric Port. If more than one loop master (FL Port) is used, one will remain inactive (be wasted) until such time as the original FL port fails. At first release, the Fibre Channel Switch will only support EMC disk arrays. Other models of disk arrays, and other mass storage will be supported at a later date. One example is shown below.

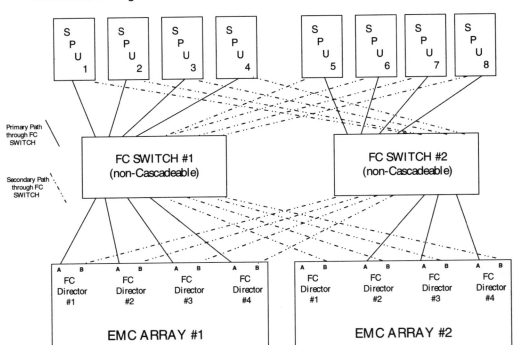

Figure 5-26   Example of FC Switch Configuration

The Gigabit Fibre Channel Switch operates as multiple channels, and is capable of providing up to eight concurrent connections. Each connection is capable of operating at the full 1 Gigabit speed. This is a significant improvement as current solutions have a single loop, which has a total speed of 1 Gigabit, which is shared between all of the attached devices.

The Gigabit Fibre Channel Switch will allow a higher transfer rate, while providing a bridge between the current Fibre Channel solutions customers have bought, and providing a link to the capabilities to be offered in the future. The Gigabit Fibre Channel Switch initially will be supported in many configurations, but will be restricted, for support reasons, to no more than two switches (not cascaded) per cluster/configuration.

There also will be a limit of no more than eight HOSTs allowed per pair of switch connections. This allows for a High Availability (HA) redundant path configuration to maximize the availability of the host systems and mass storage. See Figure 5-26. The switch will allow connection of many legacy Fibre Channel devices, but the initial release will target the EMC disk arrays and the new Hewlett-Packard Fibre Channel disk arrays.

Other mass storage will be announced as testing is completed. The configurations that will become available in the topologies using the switch become very complicated, very quickly. As such complexity is inherent with the switch, it is strongly advised that ANY configurations not specified in the HP-UX Servers Configuration Guide NOT BE IMPLEMENTED AT ANY SITE.

The Hewlett-Packard research lab, in conjunction with all of its partners, is certifying configurations as rapidly as possible for as many peripherals as possible.

The Gigabit Fibre Channel Switch will also utilize Hewlett-Packard's Fibre Channel Manager to provide configuration and Fibre Channel cluster management. The Fibre Channel Manager is a separate product, and has several requirements associated with its use, such as a workstation or other server to act as the monitoring terminal. The Gigabit Fibre Channel Switch will also interface with the Hewlett-Packard Fibre Channel Monitor program to provide proactive monitoring of events which could impact the operation of the system(s) attached to the Fibre Channel switch (exact release date of the Fibre Channel Monitor program is not yet fixed).

5.10 Typical Hewlett-Packard FC Topologies

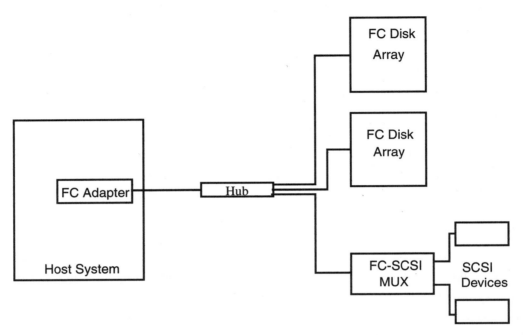

Figure 5-27   Hewlett-Packard FC Mass Storage Topology

This topology demonstrates how to attach to one host, using one I/O adapter, four mass storage devices, for example two Fibre Channel disk arrays and two SCSI tape devices, possibly DLT tape libraries, through a hub.

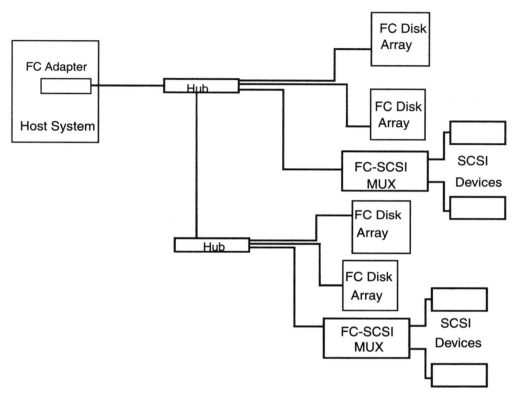

Figure 5-28 Hewlett-Packard FC Mass Storage Topology

This topology demonstrates a possible configuration using two hubs. Looking at the diagram, remember a long-wave hub has one hub-to-hub port, leaving nine other ports for devices. So you can see more possibilities with more devices.

Remember also that just because there aremultiple disk arrays and multiple other SCSI devices, and the possibility of many more devices being attached to the hubs, this is not a high availability configuration. In this particular topology there are a couple of single points of failure.

For example, there is only one FC adapter. If it fails the host will not be able to communicate with any device in the entire storage area network (SAN). The cable from the FC adapter to the first hub is also a single point of failure.

5.10.1 Year 2000 Issues

All Hewlett-Packard enterprise storage devices are Year 2000 compliant when configured according to Hewlett-Packard standards. Year 2000 compliance applies to disk drives, disk arrays, tape drives, tape libraries, magneto-optical devices, and Fibre Channel infrastructure products. All products are compliant in the original revisions shipped by Hewlett-Packard except for the Model 12 and Model 12H. The Model 12 and 12H have logging utilities that require a patch to make them Year 2000 compliant. Minimum patch revisions are shown below.

Model 12 and Model 12H Minimum Patch Revisions for Year 2000 compliance Operating System Minimum Patch Revision:
HP-UX 10.01, 10.10, 10.20PHCO_14584
HP-UX 11.0PHCO_14585
NT 4.0 SP3AutoRAID for NT version 1.02

For more information on specific products refer to the Hewlett-Packard Year 2000 Website at http://hpweb.y2k.nafohq.hp.com

Fibre Channel Futures

This chapter discusses:

- **Future developments and improvements of Fibre Channel**
- **Where to get more information regarding Fibre Channel**

6.1 Future Enhancements

Fibre Channel is evolving rapidly and new elements are constantly being defined. These new elements will produce a more powerful architecture to support mass storage.

Most of the work thus far in defining the Fibre Channel standards has been in the Fibre Channel physical standard (FC-PH). Although there will be more work done in this area, the larger amount of work in defining standards will be done in the FC-3 and FC-4 levels.

6.1.1 What Lies Ahead

6.1.1.1   Faster Fiber Rates.

The faster Fibre Channel rates of 2-plus Gbps and 4-plus Gbps are still theoretical. When implemented, however, they could greatly increase throughput. Since Hewlett-Packard supports Fibre Channel as part of it's future technology, it is continuing to produce chips and other components to support the faster rates of data transfer.

6.1.1.2   Hunt Groups

More and better definitions of hunt groups and how they will or should operate. Hunt groups could increase throughput by sending frames to an alternate port on a node, eliminating the possibility of a busy N_Port blocking communication.

6.1.1.3   Multicast Groups

As discussed in the FC-3 Common Services section of Chapter Two, the FC-3 level allows a single information unit to be transmitted to multiple N_Ports on a node. Multicast groups then could increase throughput by efficiently replicating frames to be sent to multiple N_Ports. This is roughly equivalent to a person using broadcast voice mail or email distribution lists.

6.1.1.4 Classes of Service

Newer classes of service will be added. They may address voice or video, which will offer new communication possibilities while placing new demands on the architecture.

6.1.1.5 Other Possible Enhancements

Other enhancements may address problems in the FC-AL standard or may come in the area of network management improvement. The following list includes some of the other possible improvements.

- Improved flow control
- Low-level error recovery
- Spatial reuse — more than one conversation on the loop at one time
- Full frame buffering
- Network management
    - identification of topology
    - discovery of topology when loop configuration changes
- Faster ULP error recovery
- Low-cost switching hubs

Even though these enhancements may be coming, Hewlett-Packard is only committed to the currently defined standards.

6.2 Sources for More Information Regarding Fibre Channel

6.2.1 Publications

Currently there are two major publications for introducing Fibre Channel.

1. FIBRE CHANNEL: Connection to the Future
   Fibre Channel Association
   12407 MoPac Expressway North 100-257
   P.O. Box 9700
   Austin, Texas 78766-8422

2. What is FIBRE CHANNEL
   Ancot Corporation
   115 Constitution Drive
   Menlo Park, CA 94025

6.2.2 World Wide Web

More information can be found at the following Web sites.
- http://www.x3.org
- http://www.amdahl.com/ext/CARP/FCA
- http://www.skipstone.com
- http://www.ssaia.org

(Each of these sites has links to many more associated sites.)

Glossary

Adapter   A printed circuit assembly which transmits user data (I/Os) between the host system's internal bus and the external Fibre Channel link and vice versa. Also called an I/O adapter, host adapter, or FC adapter.

Address   The logical location of a peripheral device, node, or any other unit or component in a network. The formatted number specifying a specific network location. See *SCSI Addressing*.

Arbitrated Loop   See *Fibre Channel Arbitrated Loop*.

Area   The second byte of the N_Port Identifier.

Attenuation   The difference (loss) between transmitted and received power, due to the transmission loss through equipment lines or other communications devices.

Bandwidth   The range of frequencies that can pass over a given circuit. Generally, the greater the bandwidth, the more information that can be sent through the circuit in a given amount of time.

Baud   The encoded bit rate per second. A measure of transmission speed.

Bus   A means of transferring data between modules and adapters or between an adapter and SCSI devices. For a SCSI bus definition, see *SCSI Bus*.

Cascaded FC-AL Hubs   One FC-AL hub connected to another FC-AL hub to increase arbitrated loop distances. Cascaded hubs allow distances up to 10 Kilometers between hubs, or 500 meters between a hub and a device.

Class of Service   The types of services provided by the Fibre Channel topology and used by the communicating port.

Domain   The most significant byte in the N_Port Identifier for the FC device. It is not used in the FC-SCSI hardware path ID. It is required to be the same for all SCSI targets logically connected to an FC adapter.

Fabric   A Fibre Channel term that describes a crosspoint switched network, which is one of three existing Fibre Channel topologies. A fabric consists of one or more fabric elements, which are switches responsible for frame routing. The fabric structure is transparent to the devices connected to it and relieves them of the responsibility for station management.

FC-AL   See *Fibre Channel Arbitrated Loop (FC-AL)*.

FC-AL device   A device that uses Fibre Channel Arbitrated Loop, which consists of one or more NL_Ports.

FC-AL Port   The port on the FC-AL hub that provides connection between the FC-AL adapter and the FC-AL link.

FC-SCSI Hardware Path ID   A list of values showing the physical hardware path of the host to the target device.
Format:
`Bus_Converter/Adapter_Address.Protocol_Type.Area.`
`Port.Bus.Target.LUN`
Example: 8/4.8.0.0.2.4.0

Fiber   See *Fibre Optic Cable*.

Fiber Optics   A technology that uses light as an information carrier. Fiber optic cables are a direct replacement for conventional coaxial cable and wire pairs. The glass-based transmission facility occupies less physical volume for an equivalent transmission capacity, and the fibers are immune to electrical interference.

Fibre   A generic Fibre Channel term used to cover all transmission media specified in the Fibre Channel Physical Layer standard (FC-PH), including optical fibre, copper twisted pair, and copper coaxial cable.

Fibre Optic Cable   An optical fibre cable made from thin strands of dielectric material, such as glass, through which data in the form of light pulses is transmitted by laser or LED. Fibre optic cable is used for high-speed transmission over medium to long distances.

Fibre Channel   Logically, Fibre Channel is a bidirectional, full-duplex, point-to-point, serial data channel structured for high performance capability. Physically, Fibre Channel interconnects devices, such as host systems and servers, FC hubs and disk arrays, through ports, called N_Ports, in one of three topologies: a point-to-point link, an arbitrated loop, or a crosspoint switched network, which is called a fabric. FC can interconnect two devices in a point-to-point topology, from two to 126 devices in an arbitrated loop.

FC is a generalized transport mechanism that has no protocol or native I/O command set, but can transport any existing protocol, such as SCSI, in FC frames. FC is capable of operating at speeds of 100 MB/s (full speed), 50 MB/s (half speed), 25 MB/s (quarter speed), or 12.5 MB/s (eighth speed), over distances of up to 100 m over copper media or up to 10 km over optical links. The disk array operates at full speed.

Fibre Channel Arbitrated Loop (FC-AL)   One of three existing Fibre Channel topologies, in which two to 126 ports are interconnected serially in a single loop circuit. Access the FC-AL is controlled by an arbitration scheme. The FC-AL topology supports all classes of service and guarantees in-order delivery of FC frames when the originator and responder are on the same FC-AL. The disk array's default topology is arbitrated loop.

Fibre Channel Arbitrated Loop Hub   A full-duplex, 1.063 Gigabit per second intelligent hub used in a FC-AL topology to increase the loop's reliability, the number of loop connections, and the distances between the host system(s) and disk array(s). A maximum of ten devices can be connected to each FC-AL hub.

Fibre Channel Protocol for SCSI (FCP)   FCP defines a high-level Fibre Channel mapping layer (FC-4) that uses lower-level Fibre Channel (FC-PH) services to transmit SCSI command, data, and status information between a SCSI initiator and a SCSI target across the FC link using FC frame and sequence formats.

Frame   A collection of bits that contain both control information and data; the basic unit of transmission on a network. Control information is carried in the frame with the data to provide for such functions as addressing, sequencing, flow control, and error control to the respective protocol levels. It can be of fixed or variable length.

The smallest, indivisible unit of application-data transfer used by Fibre Channel. Frame size depends on the hardware implementation and is independent of the application software. Frames begin with a 4-byte Start of Frame (SOF), end with a 4-byte End of Frame (EOF), include a 24-byte frame header and a 4-byte Cyclic Redundancy Check (CRC), and can carry a variable data payload from 0 to 2112 bytes, the first 64 of which can be used for optional headers.

Gigabit Link Module (GLM)   A physical component that manages the functions of the FC-0 layer, which are the physical characteristics of the media and interface, including driver, transceivers, connectors, and cables. Also referred to as a Physical Link Module (PLM).

Host   In the context of peripheral devices, a processor that runs an operating system using a disk array for data storage and retrieval.

Hub   A repeater used to connect several nodes in a network. A hub is a concentration point for data and repeats data from one node to all other connected nodes.

LED   Light emitting diode.

Light Emitting Diode   A small light on a device that is often used to provide status information.

Link   In Fibre Channel, it is two unidirectional fibres transmitting in opposite directions and their associated transmitters and receivers that serve as the communication media between nodes in a topology. Comparable to a bus in the SCSI protocol.

Long Wave   Lasers or LEDs that emit light with wavelengths around 1300 nm. Long wave lasers are used for long Fibre Channel links, from approximately 700 to 10,000 m. They are typically used with single-mode fiber of a 9 micron core size.

Loop Address   The unique ID of a node in Fibre Channel loop topology, sometimes referred to as a Loop ID.

Loop Port (L_Port)   An N_Port or F_Port that supports arbitrated loop functions associated with arbitrated loop topology.

N_Port   A "Node" port. A Fibre Channel defined hardware entity that performs data communication over the Fibre Channel link. It is identifiable by a unique Worldwide Name. It can act as an originator or a responder.

N_Port Identifier   A unique address identifier by which an N_Port is uniquely known. It consists of a Domain (most significant byte), an Area, and a Port, each 1 byte long. The N_Port identifier is used in the Source Identifier (S_ID) and Destination Identifier (D_ID) fields of a Fibre Channel frame.

Node   A physical device that allows for the transmission of data within a network.

Originator   The Fibre Channel N_Port responsible for starting and exchange. Fibre Channel term for a SCSI initiator.

Point-to-point   One of three existing Fibre Channel topologies, in which two devices are directly connected by a link with no fabric, loop, or switching elements present.

Port   The hardware entity that connects a device to a Fibre Channel topology. A device can contain one or more ports.

Protocol   Formal set of rules governing the format, timing, sequencing, and error control of exchanged messages on a data network; may also include facilities for managing a communications link and /or contention resolution. A protocol may be oriented toward data transfer over an interface, between two logical units directly connected, or on an end-to-end basis between two end users over a large and comple network. Both hardware protocols and software protocols can be defined.

RAID   Redundant Array of Independent Disks. A method for configuring multiple disk modules into a logical disk unit, which appears to the host system as a single, contiguous disk module.

RAID-0   Three or more disk modules bound as striped disks (the disk array reads and writes file information with more than one disk at a time). RAID-0 offers enhanced performance by using simultaneous I/O to different modules, but does not intrinsically offer high availability. For high availability, the striped disks can be software mirrored. RAID-0 is not supported and can be accessed only in FE mode.

RAID-1 Even numbers of mirrored disk modules.

RAID-1/0 A RAID configuration in which four, six, eight, ten, twelve, fourteen, or sixteen disk modules are bound as a mirrored RAID-0 group. The disk modules are mirrored such that one half the disk modules contain user data and the other half contain a disk-by-disk copy of the user data. A RAID-1/0 group combines the speed advantage of RAID-0 with the redundancy advantage of mirroring.

RAID-3 A RAID-3 group in a Hewlett-Packard High Availability Fibre Channel Disk Array must consist of exactly five disk modules, each on a separate internal SE SCSI-2 bus. RAID-3 uses disk striping and a dedicated parity disk, but not hardware mirroring.

RAID-5 A RAID configuration in which from three to sixteen disk modules use disk striping, with high availability provided by parity information distributed on each disk module. The ideal number of disk modules in a RAID-5 group is five.

Responder The logical function in an N_Port responsible for supporting the exchange initiated by the originator in another N_Port. Fibre Channel term for a SCSI target.

SCSI Small Computer System Interface. An industry standard for connecting peripheral devices and their controllers to a processor.

SCSI Addressing A fast/wide SCSI adapter supports up to 16 devices, including itself. Each device has its own unique SCSI address. The SCSI address of a device dictates the devices's priority when arbitrating for the SCSI bus. SCSI address "7" has the highest priority. The next highest priority address is "6" followed by 5, 4, 3, 2, 1, 0, 15, 14, 13, 12, 11, 10, 9, 8, with "8" being the lowest priority address. The fast/wide SCSI adapter is factory set to address "7."

A narrow SCSI adapter supports up to eight devices, including itself. SCSI address "7" has the highest priority followed by 6, 5, 4, 3, 2, 1, and 0.

SCSI Port   An opening at the back of the SCSI MUX providing connection between the SCSI adapter and the SCSI bus.

Shortwave   Lasers or LEDs that emit light with wavelengths around 780 nm or 850 nm. Short wave lasers are used for Fibre Channel links up to approximately 700 m. They are typically used with multimode fibre. The preferred fibre core size is 50 microns since this fibre has large bandwidth so that the distance is limited by the fibre attenuation. A 62.5 micron core size is also supported for compatibility with existing FDDI installations. Fibre of this type has smaller bandwidth and, in this case, the distance is limited by the fibre bandwidth.

SP   See *Storage-Control Processor (SP)*.

Storage-Control Processor (SP)   A printed-circuit board with memory modules that control the disk modules in the storage system chassis. The SP runs Grid Manager, which is used to bind and unbind logical disk units, set up disk array caching, observe array status, and view the SP event log. The SP in a disk array divides the multiplexed SCSI-2 bus traffic from the host into five internal, single-ended, SCSI-2 buses (identified by the letters A, B, C, D, and E). Each internal SCSI-2 bus supports multiple logical disk units (LUNs).

Topology   The physical layout of devices on a network. The three Fibre Channel topologies are fabric, arbitrated loop, and point-to-point. The disk array's default topology is arbitrated loop.

Bibliography

References

1. Smith, Judith A. and Maris Montanet. "Tachyon: A Gigabit Fibre Channel Protocol Chip." *Hewlett-Packard Journal,* Vol. 47, no. 5, October 1996, pp. 99–111.
2. Fibre Channel Association. *FIBRE CHANNEL Connection to the Future.* Publication Services, Bookmark, SanDiego, CA, 1994. ISBN: 1-878707-19-1.
3. Dedek, Jan and Gary Stephens. *What is FIBRE CHANNEL?* ANCOT Corporation, Menlo Park, CA, 1996.
4. Hewlett-Packard. *Hewlett-Packard Fibre Channel Mass Storage Adapters.* Hewlett-Packard Company, 1997.
5. Hewlett-Packard. *Fibre Channel SCSI Multiplexer.* Hewlett-Packard Company, 1997.
6. Hewlett-Packard. *Hewlett-Packard Fibre Channel Arbitrated Loop Hub.* Hewlett-Packard Company, 1997.
7. Hewlett-Packard. *Hewlett-Packard High Availability Fibre Channel Disk ArrayUser's Guide.* Hewlett-Packard Company, 1997.

Index